Praise for *Lighten Up!*

*"**Lighten Up!** is vintage Loretta—hilarious and profound simultaneously. Read this and you'll laugh yourself thin!"*

— **Christiane Northrup, M.D.**, the best-selling author of
The Secret Pleasures of Menopause and
Women's Bodies, Women's Wisdom

"Loretta does a masterful job in helping us bust a gut while we attempt to lose ours. The book is a treasure trove of humor, generous self-reports, and the latest in scientific information cobbled together in a funny flow. We will all be lighter for it."

— **John Ratey, M.D.**, clinical associate professor
of psychiatry, Harvard Medical School; co-author of
Driven to Distraction; and author of *Spark:
The Revolutionary New Science of Exercise and the Brain*

*"In her classic wise and witty style, Loretta LaRoche's
Lighten Up! will help all kinds of people find a sensible
and enjoyable way to get back to good health. It gives
people the commonsense solutions they need to
begin to enjoy their meals and get healthy."*

— **Miriam E. Nelson, Ph.D.**, university professor and
best-selling author of *Strong Women Stay Young*

*"People tend to lose their sense of humor when faced with
the prospect of eating well and losing weight. But I have to say
that Loretta has done it again—she actually makes the topic fun.
She helps you giggle while you lose your middle."*

— **Alice D. Domar, Ph.D.**, executive director,
Domar Center for Mind/Body Health; and
author of *Be Happy Without Being Perfect*

Lighten Up!

Other Hay House Titles by Loretta LaRoche

The Best of Loretta LaRoche (4-CD set)

How to Be a Wild, Wise, and Witty Woman:
Making the Most Out of Life Before You Run Out of It (4-CD set)

Juicy Living, Juicy Aging: Kick Up Your Heels . . .
Before You're Too Short to Wear Them (book)

Life Is Short—Wear Your Party Pants: Ten Simple Truths That Lead
to an Amazing Life (available as a book, 2-CD set, and a DVD)

Relax—You May Only Have a Few Minutes Left: Using the Power
of Humor to Overcome Stress in Your Life and Work (book)

Squeeze the Day: 365 Ways to Bring JOY and JUICE
into Your Life (book)

The Wise and Witty Stress Solution Kit

All of the above are available at your local
bookstore, or may be ordered by visiting:

Hay House USA: **www.hayhouse.com**®
Hay House Australia: **www.hayhouse.com.au**
Hay House UK: **www.hayhouse.co.uk**
Hay House South Africa: **www.hayhouse.co.za**
Hay House India: **www.hayhouse.co.in**

Lighten

Up!

The Authentic and Fun Way to Lose Your Weight and Your Worries

Loretta LaRoche

HAY HOUSE, INC.
Carlsbad, California • New York City
London • Sydney • Johannesburg
Vancouver • Hong Kong • New Delhi

Published and distributed in the United States by: Hay House, Inc.: www
.hayhouse.com • **Published and distributed in Australia by:** Hay House
Australia Pty. Ltd.: www.hayhouse.com.au • **Published and distributed in the
United Kingdom by:** Hay House UK, Ltd.: www.hayhouse.co.uk • **Published
and distributed in the Republic of South Africa by:** Hay House SA (Pty), Ltd.:
www.hayhouse.co.za • **Distributed in Canada by:** Raincoast: www.raincoast
.com • **Published in India by:** Hay House Publishers India: www.hayhouse
.co.in

Editorial supervision: Jill Kramer • *Design:* Tricia Breidenthal

Library of Congress Cataloging-in-Publication Data

LaRoche, Loretta.
  Lighten up! : the authentic and fun way to lose your weight and your
worries / Loretta LaRoche.
    p. cm.
  ISBN 978-1-4019-2157-6 (hardcover : alk. paper) 1. Weight loss. 2. Food
habits--Psychological aspects. 3. Reducing diets--Evaluation. 4. Stress
(Psychology)--Prevention. I. Title.
  RM222.2.L342 2010
  613.2'5--dc22
                                        2008047369

ISBN: 978-1-4019-2157-6

12 11 10 09   4 3 2 1
1st edition, August 2009

Printed in the United States of America

To all of us who have lost
and gained a tribe of people.
May we gain more access
to our hearts than
to our stomachs.

Contents

Introduction

"The first thing you lose on a diet is your sense of humor."

— Anonymous

As I sit down to begin writing this book, I have to wonder: *What possesses me to want to deal with a subject that has thousands of books written about it already? What else is there to say? And is there anything I can add to the dialogue that's really new?*

One of the reasons why I feel compelled to write this book is simple: I can't stand it anymore! The other is the desire to encourage you to develop a more pragmatic and optimistic approach in relation to food, movement, and life's inevitable ups and downs.

Weight loss, exercise, and stress management have become a national mania—the holy trinity of daily conversation. Virtually all of us spend precious time with our friends going on and on about food, exercise, or our overwhelming schedules. Every magazine (certainly those aimed at women) screams from its cover about new diet secrets, ways to be happy, or how to slow down. And those articles are juxtaposed with ones about how we can look thinner in our clothes without dieting, recipes that feature fried chicken or cream pies, and ideas on how to do more in less time. I suppose that the editorial staff is trying to please as many readers as possible, but it can make one a little nuts.

In addition, we listen to newscasters who are constantly reporting scientific research on health, but the problem is that they want to report on everything that sounds interesting or provocative, even if a study has gone on for all of two minutes. We need to keep in mind that these findings aren't always ready to bear fruit—one of the primary mottoes of academics is "Publish or perish."

For example, right now blueberries are at the top of researchers' lists, with supposed evidence that you could live longer (and even have improved memory so you can remember that you did) if you eat at least a half cup every day. But that could easily change in the next few months and be replaced by bug juice. Gluten, on the other hand, is on its way to becoming the Antichrist. The end result of all the overreporting is mass confusion, which usually leads to a lot of people throwing their hands up and exclaiming, "The hell with all of it!"

Eating well, being fit, and learning to relax are at the core of living a healthy, vital life. But how did we as a culture grow so fat and become so tense over such a short period of time? Much of my work deals with stress management, and so do my previous books. I've chosen to focus on weight and its negative effects in this one because the topic has become such a national obsession. We cannot overlook the implications that anxiety has on weight gain, but it's not the whole enchilada. How did we simultaneously seem to grow more knowledgeable and aware about every molecule that passes our lips—including its calorie, cholesterol, fiber, and polyunsaturated-fat counts—yet most of us keep growing fatter and fatter?

The Lean Years

When I was a young child, it was unusual to see a really large person. Sure, there were some chunky people around, but it was rare to see someone who was morbidly obese.

My grandparents lived through the Depression and World War II when food was a bit harder to come by. Because people were forced to ration, it was difficult to overeat and get fat. There were no such things as deep-dish three-meat pizzas oozing with cheese, 32-ounce cola drinks, or ice-cream cones big enough to use as signals for highway construction. People were lucky to have a little bit of chicken, a piece of bread, and some soup.

Was there something about those years of deprivation that turned the subsequent generations into fatter versions of their relatives? Did we somehow alter our DNA, creating an inability to control our food intake because we feared there wouldn't be enough to go around?

Growing up, my family was big on beans, rice, vegetables, fruit, and pasta. Desserts were a rarity. Modern conveniences certainly weren't available, so calorie expenditure was much greater. Today we've allowed ourselves to become immobilized by our cars and gadgets. We barely move unless we have to. I'm surprised that people haven't mutated into beings with wheels instead of legs.

And one of the most significant differences between the former and present generations is the mass addition of sugar and high-fructose corn syrup to our foods. The typical American consumes 140 to 150 pounds of the sweet stuff per year. We've become "sweetoholics." There's a great deal of evidence to support the fact that these substances elevate insulin levels, which in turn make it easier to get fat and stay fat. We're also at the mercy of a society that wants what they want, when they want it—in other words, live for today, eat it all, and diet tomorrow.

The Era of Consumption

On top of that, we find ourselves the target of advertisers who try to entice us into buying food by the bushel. They achieve this by tapping into our every desire. Everywhere we turn there's an enormous photograph of a rich, enticing chocolate cake; a triple latte; or a huge steak surrounded by all things fried. And we also have to add the all-you-can-eat specials for $2.99—we're into value for our dollars. Of course we're fat! How could we not be? Our nature is stacked against us—as well as very powerful national food industries.

Mother Nature did provide us with a stop sign that says, "Hello, you're full!" in the form of a hormone called *leptin,* but for most, it's all too easy to override it. This is one way in which Mother Nature lets us down. In fact, she's working against us these days because our programming to overeat is so susceptible to the temptations of the food industry, which encourages us to go ahead and indulge. And worse, we're especially drawn to items that are filled with fat and sugar because they stay with us and give us energy reserves to deal with our stressed-out lives. Our brains haven't caught up with the 21st-century lifestyle; and it may be centuries yet before they do. Unlike everything else in the world these days, evolution takes its own sweet time.

At this point in history, it's estimated that Americans are collectively overweight by five billion pounds. Five billion! Talk about supersized! It's a problem of titanic proportions. We're all concerned about the size of our waistlines, but what many of us don't think about is how the collective weight problem burdens everyone.

Diseases and chronic conditions related to obesity tax the health-care system enormously, including costs for diabetes treatment, high-blood-pressure medication, cholesterol-lowering drugs, knee surgery, and on and on. Plus, think about the future and how many millions of men and women with these medical conditions will need assistance from their friends or family members just to get through the everyday tasks in their lives. I often want to tell people that it's one thing not to care about their own health—but don't they care about their loved ones who will need to carry them and their oxygen tank around for years to come?

I'm Not Afraid of Heights, Just Widths

This book wouldn't resonate with authenticity if I'd been Ms. Slenderella my entire life. Most of us bond when we feel we've walked down the same path, and believe me, I've worn down the path of weight struggle to particles of dust. My own tale of woe up and down the slope of yo-yo dieting may sound familiar. As a preteen, I suddenly started putting on pounds. And like so many, the reason was because my home life was rife with anxiety, which led to an incredible struggle to feel good about myself.

My first seven years were spent in the embrace of my grandparents in Brooklyn. Love, laughter, and lasagna were the basics of everyday life. I was a normal little kid who weighed just the right amount. There were three meals a day, and occasionally there was a snack—maybe a piece of fruit or biscotti with a latte. (Yes, I was allowed light coffee, which wasn't unusual in those days. Maybe that's why I turned out so short.)

Both of my grandparents loved to cook and owned a bakery/spaghetti store before my grandfather had to stop working because of a disability. Their love of good food created an environment in which meals and cooking were a central part of each day. Many of us today may think that such care and attention to detail is a symptom of a psychotic disorder—however, it was wonderful. My grandparents went to the market every day and brought back fresh vegetables, fruit, and a little bit of meat. Meat was never the focal point of the meal; it merely enhanced it. Once they returned with the groceries, no matter what my grandparents planned to cook, it always felt like we were in the midst of filming a movie. Neighbors would stop by and sit and watch the drama (or comedy) unfold. And I was always given a bit part, whether it was stirring the sauce or tasting one of the dishes so they'd get my approval. I never thought of food as anything but fun and sustenance.

After we ate, there was always the after-dinner stroll, which was when my grandparents would go over the day's activities and gossip. The primary reason to walk according to them was to aid digestion, not for aerobic conditioning. Exercise was what they did all day. They never sat down or changed their shoes depending on the activity. They moved from one task to another seamlessly. Today that's called cross-training.

Unfortunately, all of that would soon change, and it would mark the beginning of my lifelong struggle with weight. The transition occurred when my mother decided, ironically, to move to the suburbs because she thought it would be better for me and her new husband. My grandparents moved to their own place, and I was left with my mother and stepfather, both of whom worked and had a very strained, dysfunctional relationship. I became a latchkey kid—my primary nurturers, my grandparents, had disappeared. Our eating patterns changed, and the socialization I'd gotten from all the old eccentric Italians who stopped by had vanished, too. I remember feeling very lonely, and I began snacking more in order to stem some of the sadness. I didn't eat a lot, because my stepfather knew exactly what was in our pantry and refrigerator and would have thought nothing of embarrassing me if he'd noticed my overeating. But all it takes is an additional couple of hundred calories a day to start the shift. I slowly started to gain weight.

I was never morbidly obese, just "chubby," as it was called in my day. Yet my mother has never been one to communicate with empathy. She goes right for the jugular, or in this case, the butt. She'd make comments like, "You're starting to look like an egg" or "I don't think we can shop in the regular teen department anymore." I was mortified. But she wasn't interested in how my self-esteem would fare as she spoke her version of the truth. Her only goal was to get me to recognize that I had gained weight, and she didn't like it.

Well, I didn't like it either. Who likes being fat? And what can be worse than being a preteen with big boobs, as the boys point at you and rub against you when they walk by? I wanted to be looked at in the way that Julie Schmidt was— my blonde, slim, blue-eyed classmate. I was the ethnic opposite: dark eyes and hair and an overly curvy body.

I remember around this time I had a pair of woolen pants that I loved, but the thighs rubbed together in such a way that it sounded like birds were chirping between my legs. It got worse and worse until the thighs were almost worn out entirely, but my grandmother said, "Don't worry, I can fix them!" So she took my pants and gave them back to me a few days later with leather patches sewed on the inner thighs. Her intentions were loving, but I was morti-fied. What did she think I was going to do with these . . . be in a rodeo?

The pièce de résistance came when my mother took me shopping for school clothes in the "Chubbette Department." I was so embarrassed! I kept hiding behind mannequins, which were also on the heavy side, hoping that no one would see me. But of course, one of the other unlucky chubbies in my class was there at the same time. Unfortunately for me, he was not only overweight, but he also suffered from a big mouth. His sense of self wasn't compromised by his added girth, and he blabbed about our encounter in the fat depart-ment all over school. We're all aware of how cruel kids can be sometimes, so you can imagine the sort of harassment I got. I now not only had to deal with my mother's vitriolic com-ments, but she also had a verbal mafia at my school to back her up.

This propelled me into a lifelong journey of self-loathing, depending on what size or shape my body was in. I was always on a search for the right diet or the best exercise rou-tine. While I was carrying my second child, I ballooned to 170 pounds. Eating became my primary drive. No matter where I went, I'd make sure I had a sandwich with me. I had to wear flip-flops because my toes were too fat to fit into my shoes.

Right after I delivered, my doctor put me on what were then called "black beauties," or amphetamines. Speed really takes off weight, but it also makes you so wired you become the Energizer Bunny. I could have maintained an entire office building by myself. Forget sleeping—your mind never stops whirring. Believe it or not, this experience was common in those days. My physician wasn't concerned about the side effects because he said that if it got too bad, I could always take Valium.

At the end of three months, I'd lost all the weight but was also a nervous wreck and suffered from panic attacks. I ended up actually having to take Valium, which slowed down my body and precipitated my wanting to eat more than I should have. (The irony of all this angst was the fact that I was probably only about 20 pounds over my ideal weight—which wasn't a big deal. But my ability to counter my internal critic was practically nil.)

Over the years that followed, I kept trying to rid myself of excess weight in all the ways that were in fashion, including the Scarsdale Diet (it obviously didn't work for Jean Harris because she killed Dr. Tarnower, who created it); the cabbage-soup diet, which isn't great for social gatherings; and the Beverly Hills diet, which suggests a breakfast of eight ounces of prunes. It's interesting how many of these diets prompt lots of bathroom visits. Maybe the point is that while you're on the pot, you can't eat. These schemes only served to make me feel even more discouraged and out of touch with real issues.

Let's Get a Grip

I've watched so many participants in my workshops and seminars struggle with the same dilemma. We're seduced into believing that there's some special food, program, or individual out there who's going to save us from our "fat pants." And as our national problem has grown exponentially over the years, so has the number of people trying to make a buck off our misery and paranoia.

It's time to come to our senses and stop buying into every nitwit who appears on a talk show touting the latest, greatest fat-loss program. The only outcome seems to be that these people get rich and we stay fat. Are there actually books and programs that make sense? Absolutely! (I'll list some of them in the Resources section of this book.)

How do we slog through this mess in the meantime? It feels like we're on a never-ending spiral of overeating, diets, too much stress, and too little exercise. The result of all this confusion is a loss of connection to what is one of the primary pleasures of life and its benefits. We need to *stop* the craziness surrounding how we think about food and start creating a lifestyle that resonates with healthier values. Eating well, exercising, and managing stress levels are the gifts we've been given that make life worth living.

Finally, I believe that much of the weight gain, stress, and lack of physical activity that's so prevalent today is also the result of a society that has forgotten how to nourish itself. We're often filling up with food to counter the sense of loneliness that has crept into our lives as we've moved more and more from a culture of community to one of isolation. In my book *Juicy Living, Juicy Aging,* I used the Italian phrase *a tavola non s'invecchia,* meaning "at the table one never grows old."

But instead of enjoying our time at the table, using it as a way to share current events or learn more about each other, we engage in nutritional one-upmanship. We bandy about words that make us sound as if we're conducting experiments at Harvard Medical School. One just can't sit at the table and expound on how delicious the spaghetti and meatballs are. Someone has to interrupt with a lecture on how good the tomatoes in the sauce are for us because of the lycopene (a substance that could help prevent some cancers). And someone else will suggest that we should have used 12-grain pasta or that the meatballs should have been turkey or soy that had been hand delivered by a eunuch from Outer Mongolia.

As soon as a new scientific theory is announced about a food source, a plethora of books emerge until it becomes something capable of curing anything from warts to flatulence to dry vaginas. Then the parade of lemmings begins, as we all trudge down to the supermarket to load up.

But there is no magic bullet. Despite the latest findings and all the varied weight-loss programs available, for the most part, losing weight is still very much a conundrum that requires real work. It will take a lot more research before we have a drug that may help those who have a biological problem keeping their weight in check. And there's no pill in sight to help those who simply overeat. Right now, most individuals who have lost weight regain it (plus more) within three years—meaning that once we've gotten on the fat train, it's very hard to get off and stay off.

I've struggled with this problem, I've watched countless friends suffer because of it, and I've helped tens of thousands of people deal with the stresses that bear down on their lives, often because of weight and health issues.

The following chapters offer a variety of solutions that you might not have explored up to this point. They require taking action. These answers aren't simple, but they're much easier to incorporate into your life than expending your time and energy on useless diets, gadgets, and faux scientific cures. They take commitment, common sense, and the ability to learn emotional self-regulation—three things that aren't particularly valued in society today.

But I'm always heartened to realize that our parents' and grandparents' generations were 20 to 30 pounds thinner on average than we are now. If they could do it, we can do it. We have access to a lot more information about food and health than they ever had; but they had more discipline, more community, and fewer choices. It's time for us to start using what we know now in combination with the wisdom of the past so that we can lighten up and gain a *huge* life.

CHAPTER ONE

Food Is Neither the Enemy Nor the Savior

"You don't get a whole life just by eating whole grains."

Doesn't it seem as if every day there's another news story about how some type of food has been proven to either be surprisingly good for you (like chocolate) or surprisingly bad for you (like wheat)? There's probably a "grain" of truth in these stories, but don't you think that some of them are made to sound bigger than they are just to grab your attention and make you buy magazines or watch certain shows? It's what the media does, after all, about everything. Reporters write about food with the same overblown drama they use to cover movie stars and politics. *"Tonight at 10: acai berries. Can they really raise your IQ by 50 percent?"* If you listen to these reports too much, you start to feel like everything you eat will either save your life or kill you.

This has given all of us what is almost a Calvinistic mentality—we spend an awful lot of time chastising ourselves, making ourselves feel bad about some of the things we do to feel good. Taking a few licks from an ice-cream cone becomes (in our minds) something that we need to apologize and atone for, like adultery. You've seen it: people eat something rich or sweet and roll their eyes with a guilty smile as if to say, "Oh, I'm going to have to pay for this outrage." And then they'll come up with their penance: "I'm going to have to spend two hours at the gym tomorrow."

Remember when we'd roll our eyes with *pleasure* when we tasted something delicious? Now we do it with shame and guilt. It's nuts. Haven't we all heard people describe food as sinful, evil, or bad? Out of those three words, at least *sinful* has the good fortune to go both ways. Our ears perk up when we hear a food described as "sinfully delicious." Yet we rarely allow ourselves to enjoy something that fills us with delight; instead, we flog ourselves with self-recrimination. Even at a child's birthday party, it's not uncommon for the adults to refuse to take a piece of the cake or insist that their slice be so thin that it can barely be seen with an electron microscope. What kind of message are we sending to our kids? *There's something wrong about liking that.* That's just crazy. There's nothing wrong about enjoying a sweet treat. It's when we eat the whole cake that we have a problem.

Why did food become the enemy? How did we become so stupid as a civilization that we allowed ourselves to be brainwashed into believing that eating a piece of cake makes us the equivalent of Ted Bundy? It's a piece of cake, for God's sake!

Just as we've demonized certain items, we've also put all food so deep under the microscope that it no longer seems like something we can just naturally enjoy. If the scientific community paid half the attention to crude oil that it does to pizza oil, our cars would be getting 100 miles to the gallon by now. We're constantly bombarded with studies that tell us which foods can make us healthier and why they should be essential parts of our diets. For example, we've been told that eating salmon can help with brain function, raspberries may help reduce cancer, pomegranate juice removes warts, celery makes us hear as well as a dog, and on and on. We're given all kinds of complex statistics that state that if we eat enough of this or that, we can decrease our chances of getting cancer or heart disease or Alzheimer's . . . or even of dying an early death. I've often wondered, *If I were to eat everything that's suggested in these studies, could it be that I won't die at all?*

Then of course, the studies are often negative—warning us that eating certain foods may increase our chances of contracting a particular disease or illness. We've all heard how white flour is the devil incarnate, and carbohydrates could end the human race as we know it. Pasta? Might as well just jump into the grave right now; we're as good as dead.

I am in awe that my Italian relatives managed to live long enough to finish kindergarten. I know that not a day went by in which my grandmother didn't have a little pasta at some point, and she fed it to me constantly. If such a thing were possible, she would have given it to me intravenously. And guess what? She died at 93 with all her teeth and faculties, and she never even had to use a walker.

Meat is right up there with criminals on the "most wanted list." I'm surprised we haven't created a SWAT team to ambush restaurants like Morton's Steakhouse and send the patrons away to do hard time for ordering a juicy rib eye. Of course, I'm kidding around a bit here. Is eating a two-pound steak for dinner good for you? Well, probably not unless you're an Olympic athlete. Plus, you really should pay attention to the level of hormones in the meat products you buy. But is meat something to be vilified and feared? No! The average American consumes about 200 pounds per year. *That* is what we should fear: the fact that on average, we're each eating an entire steer. If meat is included in moderate amounts—used as more of a side dish than the massive main element of a meal—it's absolutely a fine part of a healthy diet and a terrific source of protein.

Eating small amounts of meat and fish has always been a mainstay of the Asian diet until Western fast-food restaurants infiltrated their society. The average Chinese meal has shifted drastically from consisting of grains, beans, and vegetables to one in which almost half of the calories come from cooking oils, pork, poultry, beef, mutton, fish, and dairy foods. In China, people have always been fairly lean, but now at least one-fourth of adults are overweight or obese. They're also less physically active as they move from a primarily agrarian culture to one that is more industrial.

Ah, the benefits of progress. It seems as we progress, we regress! The rate at which adult citizens there are becoming overweight is climbing faster than in all developing countries except Mexico and is greater than developed nations such as the United States, Australia, and Great Britain.

So much for the old adage: "Clean your plate! Children are starving in China."

The Food Spiritualists

I'm constantly finding myself surrounded by people who think an interesting topic of conversation is their new style of eating . . . as if they'd stumbled upon the path to salvation. First of all, why in the world do they think I'd care about what they put in their mouths?

But more infuriating is when I notice that these folks are becoming more and more obsessive and taking on a tone that appears fundamentalist in its rigidity. Their diet must be adhered to with absolute perfection and must exclude foods that they consider demonic. I call these folks "food spiritualists." Sharing a meal with these monastic types could bring you to the edge and induce some major twitching.

If you dine with a food spiritualist, you must be incredibly vigilant about what you choose from the menu. Otherwise, they'll point their bony fingers in your face and begin their professorial rants about the exact molecular composition of the entrée you've selected and how you'll die an early death from your poor choices. They're on a mission: to eat only what they consider to be "clean foods" and make sure that you do, too.

The term *clean foods* seems to have cropped up in recent years, and when I hear it mentioned, my gut reaction is to want to choke the living shit out of whoever said it. Because, let's face it—if some foods are clean, then others must be "dirty." If I choose incorrectly, I better have a mop and pail with me to clean up after my filthy self. How do these people not see how absurdly self-righteous they appear to others? *"What I eat is clean. It's too bad that you don't care as much as I do about the amount of filth you put into your body."*

I think all this brouhaha about clean foods is simply another way for people to try to exert control over their complicated, stressed-out lives. When we feel out of control, we often believe that order will help. But of course, when we attempt to overly manipulate things that are by nature somewhat complex and difficult to regulate, we create a lot of unnecessary stress. Some things just can't be controlled too much.

Are there some foods that have better nutritional elements than others? Absolutely. I'd never dispute that. And as you'll see later in this book, I have some very strong opinions based on research and experience about what and how we should be eating. But I also understand that food is an enormously flexible aspect of our lives and that our relationship with it has nutritional, emotional, and social aspects—all of which should be honored and acknowledged. It's the rigidity and self-righteousness of some people that drives me crazy.

And it gets worse. If you have the audacity to ignore the chastising of one of the members of the food spiritualists' cult and eat foods they consider dirty, don't worry. They have a solution for you. They'll recommend that you do a "master cleanse." These folks are big into cleansing their insides.

Have you ever noticed how these cleanses are often embraced by celebrity types who spend days, if not weeks, at elegant spas that have created entire regimens around this process? I met someone who went to one of these cleansing palaces because she was desperately seeking a way to monitor her food intake. She was put on a 700-calorie "program" designed to rid her body of the poisons she'd ingested as part of her unhealthy diet. Several times a day she was given a variety of fruits, vegetables, and broths made with special life-enhancing ingredients. (There's always a lot of hullabaloo about the magical components of these broths—how they're made with the most exotic herbs that were transported from deep within the Amazon and that until now they've only ever been eaten by a rare parrot that has been alive for 300 years and can whistle "The Star-Spangled Banner.") After three days, this woman was so hungry she ate the centerpiece on the table.

Of course, checking into these kinds of spas can work, but I don't believe it has to do with any "cleansing." The programs are effective, thanks to the personal trainers, chefs, and assistants. And most important, the people who spend time at these places usually are eating less and moving more often, which hastens weight loss.

Other programs contend that you should not only fast but also have a high colonic as well. (Has anyone ever had a *low* colonic?) This consists of a special technician (whom I like to think of as a pooper scooper) who has been trained to excavate the waste hanging on to the sides of your intestines. These people must be convinced that this stuff weighs a lot. I personally can think of a lot better ways to rid myself of waste matter, such as eating more fiber and exercising, but, hey, whatever floats your boat . . . or your bowels.

"The rationale for intestinal cleansing—to dislodge material adhering to the colon walls—is fundamentally mistaken. When fecal matter accumulates, it compacts into firm masses in the open interior of the colon; it does not adhere to the intestinal walls as the 'sludge' depicted in the advertisements." (Harvard Health Publications, July 22, 2008: **www.health.harvard.edu**)

If you experience fatigue, weight gain or loss, rashes, insomnia, breathing problems, irritability, or are growing warts on your nose, visit your doctor—don't go to a detox spa and embark on one of the many and generally idiotic cleansing programs.

And then there are all the insane diet plans. Over and over again, we're being told about methods guaranteed to make us lose weight, reduce stress, eliminate wrinkles, improve eyesight, tone and tighten butts . . . and possibly bring us back from the dead. Some of the "methods" are akin to being in a gulag—allowing only particular items that need to be eaten at certain times and in a certain way.

Most individuals who embark on these types of diets have great passion for them in the beginning; however, as time goes by, their enthusiasm wanes. We can't satisfy our palates on a limited menu, just like we can't get excited about having sex in the exact same way over and over. It becomes a little like watching a faucet drip! It's just plain boring. Recidivism is huge with these plans.

Let's face it. If any of these diets worked, wouldn't everyone be thin? What's really mind-blowing is that we never seem to believe what the best researchers in the field have been saying for years: *Diets don't work.* End of story. But it's not something we want to hear. Like all fairy tales, the promise of some kind of rescue by the dashing prince (or in this case, the magic diet that will make us lose weight without having to count calories or exercise) is appealing, but it isn't a realistic or healthy way to live our lives.

Where to Turn for Some Good Advice

I don't want this to be a diet book, even though I know as much about the subject as most of the so-called experts who pen nutty weight-loss plans. I don't think I should be giving advice on what anyone should or shouldn't be eating. And the truth is that what each of us should eat is a very individual thing that must be tailored to our body type, moods, fitness level, and all the other psychological issues I'm going to discuss in this book.

The trick to controlling what we eat is to be moderate in all things—which is where our bodies would go instinctively if we lived in a simpler society and had more natural lives. But we don't.

So if you need some advice on what the reasonable nutritional needs of your body are, here are some reliable places to go:

- **www.mypyramid.gov**: This is a government Website that provides tailored nutritional advice, caloric counts, and even menu plans based on the national recommended food pyramid for eating a balanced, healthy diet.

- **www.americanheart.org**: The American Heart Association's Website is full of helpful information on ways to eat more responsibly in order to lose weight and improve heart health.

- **www.webmd.com/diet**: WebMD has a ton of information and some interactive quizzes you can take to help figure out if your typical eating patterns may be taking you down a bad path. Plus, it has recommendations and calculators so that you can monitor your current shape, as well as where you'd like to be.

- **http://nhlbisupport.com/cgi-bin/chd1/ diet1.cgi**: The National Heart, Lung, and Blood Institute Website has an interactive tool that helps you calculate the approximate number of calories you eat in a day based on the list of foods you enter. Plus, it monitors other factors, including cholesterol and sodium levels. It's not a tool for weight loss per se, but it will give you a lot of information that may surprise you about what you eat on a regular basis.

Consider some of the following claims found in magazines and books, and check to see if you've believed any of them:

— *Drop 16 pounds in a week!* How is this possible unless some of your limbs are amputated? A pound is equivalent to 3,500 calories, so 16 pounds is 56,000 calories that would need to be burned in order for this claim to be valid. Running a marathon burns about 3,000 calories. Unless you can do the equivalent of running three marathons a day for a week, this ain't happenin'!

— *Lose weight with the new honey slimming plan.* Who knew that a bee could be your best friend? If sugar is touted as a problem, how can honey be okay, especially since honey has *more* calories per teaspoon than table sugar and virtually identical ingredients? I know—it's natural, so it doesn't count.

— *Attack belly bulge with 40 fat-fighting meals.* Why is the terminology always made to sound like a preparation for an imminent invasion? And why 40 meals? This reminds me of some religious fasting model—it's going to take 40 days and 40 nights. Once I complete the program, am I saved from porking up for eternity?

— *Get a flat belly while you sleep!* What a deal! Does this happen from a firm mattress or by someone dropping a concrete slab on your stomach? A flat belly is the result of the reduction of fat in your body and strong core muscles that you can achieve only through abdominal exercise.

The ultimate insanity is that perhaps the only thing there seems to be *more of* in the media than diet talk is cooking shows. We sit and watch shows with chefs like Paula Deen as if they're pornography—and she uses sticks of butter like they were shakes of a pepper mill. And Emeril—*pow!* A 2,000-calorie meal! These chefs and many others are now members of a celebrity-based network that has become a crucial part of most people's lives. Watching these culinary artists create their undoubtedly delicious wonders is mouthwatering entertainment. It's part of our fantasy lives!

Recently, the T.G.I. Friday's restaurant chain announced a change in their menu. They're instituting what they're calling a "right size" portion to cater to those individuals who recognize that "normal" portions served at restaurants are really abnormal. I wish them luck! The last time a big national restaurant (Ruby Tuesday) tried to cut portion sizes, they had to immediately go back to their old ways after receiving an enormous amount of complaints from their customers.

We've set up a huge conundrum for ourselves. We watch those shows that extol our innate love of good food with one hand, and with the other, we're told that any such enjoyment is not good for us and will lead us to an early grave. How did we get ourselves into this mess, and more important, how can we get ourselves out of it? Is there a way we can once again get into a sane relationship with food that nurtures us, fuels us, brings us together, and gives us joy?

Of course there is. But first we have to face the facts.

The Literary Diet Roundup

Don't be fooled by the hype! We've been flooded with glossy diet books that promise successful weight loss from eating anything our heart desires to practically starving. It all boils down to common sense, though. Here's my take on some of the more popular titles:

— *Eat Right 4 Your Type.* This book tells you what you should eat based on your blood type. It's a nice claim that people would like to believe, and it certainly has a good "scientific" feel to it. However, the experts contend that there's no evidence that this best-selling book's claim works . . . no more than a diet that says you should eat according to your hair color. The guidelines for each blood type vary, but of course, there's one piece of advice that's the same for all types: eat fewer calories to lose weight. Surprise!

— *Sugar Busters!* This book was a huge hit and sold millions of copies. It made the claim that sugar is the enemy of the modern dieter. The authors suggest cutting virtually all sugar from your diet, including the natural sugar that comes from many fruits and vegetables such as potatoes, carrots, corn, and raisins. The book even states that eating according to its rules will stop diabetes; however, scientists say there's no proof that this style of eating will have any effect on diabetes. And similar to other diets, there's only one reason why people say that they've lost weight on it: their daily calorie intake is substantially reduced.

— *The Sonoma Diet.* Sounds sexy, doesn't it? Makes one think of wine and country meals of grilled fish and vegetables . . . uh, yeah. This diet actually makes some sense. It tells us to eat more reasonable portions of foods that are healthy and allow ourselves some sweets and treats as long as we're conscious of portion size. It's about moderation and making healthy choices. Duh!

— *The New Cabbage Soup Diet.* This one has been making the rounds for years and still pops up as a quick-fix plan for folks who want to drop pounds fast. It includes eating bowls and bowls of cabbage soup each day, in addition to one or two other low-calorie items (like a banana or baked potato). Does it make you lose weight? Sure. But so would sucking on a rock. All this diet does is force you to lower your caloric intake by filling your stomach with a low-calorie, high-fiber vegetable soup. There's no magic to it, and you could get exactly the same results (and more pleasant trips to the bathroom) if you ate a similar number of calories of varied foods.

— *The Atkins Diet.* Probably the granddaddy of fad diets, this one has been with us for years and remains controversial. You can eat all the rich cheeses, meats, and fats you want—but almost no carbohydrates. People say that it works, and thousands have lost weight using this program. However, many doctors remain unconvinced and maintain that ultimately the only reason individuals lose weight is because after a while they get sick of the high-protein, high-fat foods and consume fewer calories. And some physicians say that this diet puts people at risk for stroke and heart disease. Plus, the brain needs glucose to function properly, and carbs are the easiest source to obtain it. Are any of these health risks worth losing weight? To me, it's diet Russian roulette. Why participate in something that many doctors say could be risky when the same results can be had in a healthier fashion by simply paying attention to what you eat?

— *The Shangri-La Diet.* This plan says that in order to lose weight, you need to lower your body's "set point" (the place that is your natural, comfortable weight), which is often too high on people who are overweight. The diet says that this can be accomplished by training your body to stop associating calories with flavor, and it recommends eating a couple of tablespoons of high-calorie olive oil or sugar water between meals. It also says that you can bring down the set-point effect of foods by eating bland meals or trying unfamiliar foods. Is there any proof that it works? No—it's all anecdotal and based on the author's own success claims. Nutritionists are very skeptical, too. In fact, healthy foods *do* taste good, and adding major liquid calories doesn't make sense unless you subtract more calories from elsewhere in your diet.

— *Volumetrics.* This diet is based on the very real notion that most people like to eat more than less, and it shows the difference between what the author calls "high-energy-density foods" with "low-energy-density foods." In other words, you can eat a lot more of some foods (for example, fruits and vegetables) than you can of others (meats, fats, and so forth). It seems to me that this is just another way of saying that you need to keep track of calories. High-density foods have a lot of calories, and low-density foods have fewer. Ultimately, this diet simply teaches you how to pay attention to the amount of high-calorie food you consume. Does it work? It's common sense, God bless it.

— *The South Beach Diet.* This is a more sensible version that's reminiscent of Atkins, in that it calls for a lot of protein and few carbs. However, unlike Atkins, it doesn't permit dieters to indulge in rich fats, and it does include healthier carbs (such as fruits, vegetables, and whole grains), as well as recommending reasonable portion sizes. In other words, eat less, focus on healthier vegetables and lean meats, and stay away from foods with very high fat and sugar contents. Couldn't your grandmother have told you that 20 years ago?

"Food is our common ground, a universal experience."

— James A. Beard

CHAPTER TWO

How What We Eat Begins to Eat at Us

"You've been sold a bill of goods—and have swallowed it!"

I love food as much as anyone, but even I can't deal with the size of the entrées that most restaurants consider a "portion" (which could feed a family of five). Some people use common sense to deal with this and survive with their waistlines intact because they take half their food home in a doggie bag and make another meal out of it the next day. But when those huge dishes are put in front of us, many of us eat until it's gone.

The marketing staffs of food chains understand that the best way to appeal to consumers is to give them a lot for their money. This is due to two reasons: First, much of the American public has been trained to believe that they're only getting a good value when portions border on enormous. Second, extra-large servings "feed" our internal natural drive to store up food in case of a famine. So smart marketers have used our instincts against us to get us to spend our money—even though it means that we eat more than anyone could possibly need.

> I strongly recommend the charming book *French Women Don't Get Fat* by Mireille Guiliano. Finally, a "diet" book with some common sense! The author recommends that you eat three meals a day, keep portions small, drink a little wine, buy seasonal vegetables, and go for walks. And if you have a treat now and then, good for you. Vive la France!

It's not uncommon to see ads for foot-long subs, two-pound burgers loaded with cheese and bacon, buckets of fried chicken (with fried accompaniments!), and three huge scoops of super-premium (in other words, high fat content) ice cream piled high on a chocolate-dipped cone. The people we see eating these quantities in the advertisements are always happy and laughing, with bodies as sleek as the Olympic swim team.

I'd love to one day see a commercial showing some of the *real* folks I've seen chowing down in the restaurants advertised. It isn't a pretty picture. You can virtually see their arteries screaming for help (not to mention the strained seams of their stretch clothing). Isn't it ironic that in the land of plenty, we think we need to eat a day's worth of food at one meal? Why do we feel like we have to stuff our faces as if at any moment we might be abducted and starved for weeks?

Food is available 24/7, and at some point, we started believing that we can't go without eating for more than an hour or so, if that. We've become a nation of chronic snackers. It's as if we've gone back to being infants, needing several feedings a day. We might be all set if someone invents a plastic breast that emits a formula that tastes like Whoppers.

"Never eat anything larger than your head."

— Miss Piggy

How to Read a Nutrition Label

Understanding the nutritional-facts labeling on packaged foods should be obvious, but it isn't. And like so many things, the food industry has figured out ways to be tricky and make their products appear to be healthier than they really are. I think I've made it clear that I'm not a big proponent of counting every damn thing you put in your mouth; rather, I'm for common sense. But sometimes that requires you to know what you're talking about. If you're not sure what's in the items you're buying, here's what to look for:

— *Portion size.* From my point of view, this ranks the highest in importance when reading a label. Here's where people get fooled. You buy a small bag of potato chips, and the label says that it has 180 calories with a portion size at about one ounce. *Ah, that's not so bad,* you think. But you may have missed the note above the box that says: "Number of portions per container: 3." So all of a sudden, what you thought was a 180-calorie snack has now become a 540-calorie snack. And everything else gets tripled, too. Be sure to read all of the portion information, and don't be fooled! Some breakfast cereals list single servings as 1 cup, ¾ cup, or even ½ cup. So if you look quickly and think, *Oh, they're all around 100 calories,* you may be way off if you haven't looked closely at the portion size.

— *Calories.* This should be obvious. If you want to know how much weight you're likely to gain by what you eat, you need to do a little research and figure out approximately how many calories you burn in a day. If you want to drop some pounds, then the total number of calories you eat in a day should be lower than the number of calories you burn—that's it. Badda bing, badda boom.

— *Calories from fat.* It's better to eat fewer calories from fat, but like all things, it's more important that you're conscious of what you're eating. Peanut butter is half fat but can be very healthy and shouldn't be banned from most people's diets. However, you can't eat the whole jar while sitting in front of the TV.

— *Total fat, saturated fat, trans fat, cholesterol, and sodium.* These are the items that people try to limit in their diets. If you look at the column that says "% Daily Value," that's the approximate percentage of the recommended daily amount of the item that's included in the portion being measured on the label. So if you're having a small snack, and it's 50 percent of your daily recommended amount of fat, you should probably switch to something else.

— *Total carbohydrates.* Once again, look at the percentages of the daily value. If a certain kind of food is providing you with 80 percent of your daily requirement, it probably isn't a very wise choice.

— *Dietary fiber, vitamin A, vitamin C, calcium, and iron.* Here's the good stuff. For these nutrients, you're looking for *higher,* not lower, daily percentages. But don't go overboard. You could eat 400 percent of the daily fiber requirements, but do you want every trip to the bathroom to be like woodworking class?

Remember that daily percentages are based on an adult diet of 2,000 calories per day. You may need to be eating more or less than that to lose or maintain your weight. These labels are a good way to compare and contrast foods, and to give you an idea of what you're eating. But like all things, don't go crazy.

I've gotten to the point where I now order a child's-size soda when I go to the movies because even the small adult size could double as a swimming pool for a gerbil. What's the point of that? It makes no sense to anyone except the people who sell it to you: you're willing to spend 50 cents more for something that costs about 2 cents to provide. The theater chain rakes in the dough, and you pack on as many extra calories as a cheeseburger.

The Skinny on Sizes

The only way to really get control over your weight is to eat the right amount for the number of calories that your body burns. Period. End of story.

Nobody wants to undertake the tedious task of counting calories, but one way or another, that's the only path to success. Whether you eat larger amounts of low-calorie foods or smaller amounts of high-calorie foods, it's all in getting the balance right.

But sometimes even when we pay attention to what we should be eating, we still have a distorted vision of what a healthy portion size is. Our perception has been skewed by the amounts we're served in restaurants these days. And even when we know the amounts we should be eating, it's still hard. I'm just as guilty as anyone else in being able to convince myself that just one cup of pasta can fill a tureen.

When judging portion size, here's a way to envision the right amounts:

- 1 cup is about the size of your fist.

- ½ cup looks like half a baseball.

- 3 ounces (often the recommended portion size of a piece of red meat or chicken) is about the size of a deck of cards.

- 1 ounce is the size of your thumb.

- 2 tablespoons looks like a Ping-Pong ball.

- 1 teaspoon looks like the tip of your thumb.

There are certainly pockets of society that suffer the indignities of hunger due to poverty, but many of us who can more than afford our daily bread have been seduced into believing that we need to eat the whole loaf plus the wrapping. We're not only eating our regular meals, but in between we're constantly grazing as if we were cows needing to chew our cuds. The calorie count of one of our snacks is often the equivalent of what should be a meal. As a culture, our mantra has become *More is better*. It permeates almost everything we do, so why not food, too?

It's an odd element of our current society. Nothing the recent generations have gone through has helped create this mentality. My grandparents and my parents had a right to feel this way since they endured the hardships of World War II and the Depression. But most of us with weight problems don't have to fear that there won't be enough for tomorrow. We've become creatures who feed our wants—not our needs.

The Loss of Family Meals

Let's face it: no one needs to be reminded that life has become incredibly complex. Most of the people I talk to in my workshops tell me that they feel like there's no end to what they have to do. Their work lives invade their personal time (if they ever even *have* any personal time), and their to-do lists just keep getting longer and longer.

I hardly ever hear people talk about a wonderful meal they enjoyed or that they're happy to go grocery shopping. What should be one of life's pleasures—preparing a nutritious meal that delights your taste buds—has become a huge inconvenience. Picking up prepared meals and fast food or simply sitting yourself down and eating in a restaurant is easier and takes less time, so it has almost become the default in our society. Cooking a meal at home has turned into a special-occasion event!

With so little time and so many items that are tempting and easily available, why bother cooking and serving? And now that many women work outside of the home, the old societal norm of the housewife preparing all family meals is gone. Enter Pizza Hut!

However, according to a 2007 article in *Parade Magazine* by Lynn Schnurnberger, numerous studies and reports have revealed just how crucial family dinners are in the lives of growing kids:

> Research shows that the benefits of family dinners go far beyond nutrition. A recent study from the University of Minnesota reported that teens who had regular meals with their parents had better grades and were less likely to be depressed. From Harvard came word that chances are slimmer—by 15%—that children will be overweight if they eat with their families. Researchers at Emory University found that preteens whose parents tell family stories at dinner have higher self-esteem and better peer relations during adolescence. A study from the National Center on Addiction and Substance Abuse at Columbia University showed that teens who have two or fewer family dinners per week (compared to those who have five or more) are more likely to smoke, drink and hang out with sexually active friends. And 12- and 13-year-olds with limited family dinners are a staggering six times more likely to have used marijuana.

The study also revealed that 84% of teens said they'd rather eat with their parents than alone.

When it comes to protecting our children against risky behavior, "the family dinner is more powerful than any law we can pass, any punishment we can level," says Joseph A. Califano Jr., chairman and president of the National Center on Addiction and Substance Abuse.

Everyone benefits from family meals. Longevity studies have shown that the support and sharing that goes on during sit-down meals with friends or family helps us live longer, healthier lives.

Quick Test

Q: How many calories does it take to gain a pound?
A: 3,500 more calories than you burn

That's a lot—about five pints of ice cream or 14 slices of pizza . . . *on top of* a normal day of eating. So if you're one of those people who believes that you put on five pounds because you had some fries, think again.

Food Seduction

Food advertising has become relentless and sneaky. To entice children into eating things that they probably shouldn't, we see dancing, chatting, and superhero-style sugary snacks doing everything but reaching out of the TV and pulling kids in face-first. I used to snack on M&M's as a treat, but now I worry that I might be eating a charming bright-red character who has a fine singing voice.

And for adults, the dancing candies are a little more insidious: they take the shape of attractive celebrities who tempt us in the same ways. We're supposed to feel good about a type of yogurt or cereal or even a brand of water because someone beautiful who gets to walk the red carpet or looks smart and hip has given it the thumbs-up.

Years ago, many doctors appeared in TV and radio ads promoting specific brands of cigarettes, and look where that got us. My grandmother and mother would have laughed their asses off at how people are seduced into buying something just because a famous person endorsed it. They used their common sense and ate what they intuitively knew would fuel their minds and bodies.

The darker side to marketing food these days, in my opinion, is how companies have figured out how to use scientific research as a way to convince us that their products are actually good for us. They know that we're concerned about our health so they try to use that as a way to lure us—but not always in ways that are honest. Sure, some ingredients are better for us than others. But it seems that whenever a study is conducted on a particular food that has been found to have some positive effects on our physiology, the marketing teams kick into gear to spin a grain of truth into the fountain of youth.

I highly recommend the book *Fast Food Nation* by Eric Schlosser for more detailed information on how the fast food industry exploits our natural instincts—and especially those of kids and teenagers.

The FDA determined that oatmeal helps lower cholesterol, and bingo . . . marketers went on a relentless campaign. It was then inserted into every stinking thing we eat and also added to our beauty products. I don't know whether to eat it or take a bath in it. Oatmeal mania has calmed down, but now pomegranates and salmon have become the new saviors. Everything that contains flavonoids and omega-3 fatty acids is presented as the key to keeping us fit and fabulous.

Are there possible benefits to consuming these foods? Absolutely! But are they going to extend your life if you aren't following other healthy principles such as exercising, managing stress, and being involved with friends and family? Very unlikely.

The Organic Panic

On top of all the research is the new layer of decision making that makes us all crazy: do I buy "organic" or "free range" . . . or do I just start my own farm?

When my mother retired to Hampton Bays in Long Island, New York, her favorite pastime was going to a local farm where she bought fresh eggs. She wanted them to literally go from the hen to the frying pan. I, for the most part, have been relegated to purchasing eggs in the supermarket. It used to be a pretty easy process. There were four sizes (small, medium, large, and extra large), and they came in two colors (white and brown). I never stopped for more than a few seconds to make my selection.

Over the past several years, however, an entire section of the dairy became devoted to eggs. I think I finally woke up to how ludicrous it has become when I realized that I'd spent well over 15 minutes trying to make a choice. There were seven different kinds, with some of them coming from hens that were organic and cage free. Does this mean that I'll have less stress if I eat eggs from a chicken that is less confined? There were also slightly brown, brown, dark brown, cream, and slightly soiled (very natural) eggs. I suspect in the near future that we'll see eggs from hens that have had therapy, have been exercised daily by a personal trainer, and ones that are allowed conjugal visits before laying their eggs.

That level of choice has been extended everywhere. Virtually every product available today comes in a conventional and organic variety. The organic version is always more expensive, and of course, it comes with some elitism attached. If we buy organic, then we're closer to godliness—we can lead ourselves to believe that what we're eating has come straight from Farmer Brown's silo. But is it anywhere near that clear-cut? And while we're unsure that organic food is better for us, do we even have a clear picture of what it means to be organic? Check out these facts:

— "According to its Web site, the USDA 'makes no claims that organic food is safer or more nutritious than conventionally produced foods.' Harvard nutrition experts say there is no solid evidence that organic foods in general are healthier for humans, but that organically raised meat may prevent the spread of diseases such as bovine spongiform encephalopathy, better known as mad cow disease." (Harvard Health Publications, Harvard Medical School, June 12, 2008: **www .health.harvard.edu**)

— "As food companies scramble to find enough organically grown ingredients, they are inevitably forsaking the pastoral ethos that has defined the organic lifestyle. For some companies, it means keeping thousands of organic cows on industrial-scale feedlots. For others, the scarcity of organic ingredients means looking as far afield as China, Sierra Leone, and Brazil—places where standards may be hard to enforce, workers' wages and living conditions are a worry, and, say critics, increased farmland sometimes comes at a cost to the environment." ("The Organic Myth," *BusinessWeek,* October 16, 2006)

So, in other words, while there's some truth to the fact that *organic* means that the product you're buying should be free of pesticides and certain chemicals, there is currently no evidence that they're better for you in any other way. There's also virtually no policing of the companies that call their products organic—particularly those that come from overseas.

I'm not saying you shouldn't eat organic foods if it seems right to you, but remember the old caveat: *Buyer beware.* Labels have become another way for companies to market themselves as virtuous when they might not be. And some people tend to think that when they're making the "virtuous" choice, they can then eat whatever they want and not gain weight. Of course, even when it comes to organic products, that's ridiculous.

Food Snobbery

Somewhere along the way, we seem to have decided to define ourselves by what and how we eat because it creates an aura of prestige. It sends a message that "I am in the know and you aren't." Or even more important, that "I am more virtuous and have more self-control than you." I've shared meals with people whom I wished could be put away.

One particular incident really stands out. I was asked to speak at a conference way up in Maine that had also included some very well-known New Age gurus. I'd gotten in late but was told that a few of the speakers were having dinner and that I should join them. I thought it was great because I was dying to meet them. It was close to midnight by the time we finished dinner, so we thought we might arrange breakfast with the waitress to be sent to our rooms.

Most of the folks requested fairly normal meals, except for one speaker and his wife who demanded that they have guava juice mixed with freshly squeezed oranges and organic eggs scrambled in grape-seed oil. They also needed ten-grain toast with shea butter on the side. Now it's the middle of winter in Bangor, Maine. When the waitress seemed a little unsure of the restaurant's ability to fulfill the request, the couple shook their heads in dismay and said it was impossible for them to perform without the breakfast as ordered. I left, shaking *my* head in disbelief as to how people could take themselves so seriously. And of course, this couple's message to the audience was all about flexibility and tolerance. . . .

I know from my travels in this enlightened world that sometimes folks who consider themselves more spiritually evolved act as if their way is the only way. But when they turn into arrogant jackasses in order to stay on their path, they truly become lost. I don't care if they want to eat beetle nuts from the Gobi Desert—that's their business. But making it someone else's responsibility to find it for them and to use it as a threat is just rude.

Comedian Redd Foxx said it best: "What are all those health fanatics going to do when they're lying in the hospital dying of nothing?"

Mindless Eating/Multitasking

Since much of the stress we experience makes us feel out of control, many of us eat mindlessly, which usually adds up to eating too much because our reptilian brains are telling us to keep foraging—we're not out of danger yet. And the things that are most enticing to store up on are the foods that bring us comfort, such as sugars and fats that are high in calories.

I think the most disgusting by-product of our stressed-out, fast-paced culture is how meals are eaten while we simultaneously do other things. Most individuals want to eat quickly so they can focus on activities like watching a favorite TV show or checking e-mail. I've seen people chatting on their cell phones in airports while stuffing themselves, as specks of food fly off their lips. No matter where we are now, someone is drinking, chewing, or both. Don't they realize, first of all, that munching while talking to someone in person or on the phone is less than civil—even kind of gross? I'm not talking about when people dine together—I mean when one person is chomping away while the other is just trying to hold a conversation.

Studies have shown that we're never as focused on something and aware as we should be when we're trying to do multiple things at the same time, so why do we continue? Why do we still seem to think that multitasking is a superhuman trait, rather than a subhuman one—especially where food is concerned?

Why indeed? I feel it's because we've become slaves to our schedules, and traditional sit-down meals simply get in the way. It's almost impossible to assess how much we've eaten in a day when everything melds together. It's much easier to eat unhealthily and in huge quantities when we stuff our faces while doing other things. Oftentimes, we don't even remember that we ate, so we eat again! Of course, if we would slow down, plan a meal, take a seat, and make it an event, that itself would bear some importance in the day; and we would very likely be more mindful of what it is we're eating.

Most of this kind of behavior is totally irrational. Does it make sense to drive your car while you're trying to down a hot cup of coffee? I wonder how many parents would approve of their children riding their bikes while chugging a soda. Once upon a time, folks never ate unless they were sitting at a table. Now *everything* is a table. I bet some people eat while sitting on the toilet.

Last year when I went to the south of France, I was struck by the difference in how the French approach eating. The menu was presented, the waitperson explained some of the dishes, and then a basket of wonderful bread was placed on the table along with butter and olive oil. I was able to listen to the other diners who were exalting in their delight of the warm, crusty bread. I didn't hear anyone saying that it was evil, as if it were the spawn of an alien invasion. I also saw people enjoying pasta, potatoes, and other foods that we (Americans) blame our weight gain on.

No one asked for the sauces to be put on the side or underneath or next to the dish. And no one requested a green salad instead of the accompanying side dish. The patrons enjoying their lovely meals weren't heavy or bloated, and didn't look like they needed to go into rehab. I asked our waiter how many of his customers made special modifications to their orders. He answered that very few do since it's considered a slight to the chef in their culture.

One thing noticeably different was the size of the portions—small compared to ours—and also the long amounts of time people took to eat. Dining in Europe is leisurely and considered part of the "good life."

Interestingly, I also never witnessed anyone walking down the street eating. Cafés abound, and people actually take the time to stop and sip cappuccinos and chat with their companions or simply observe their surroundings. In the U.S., on the other hand, we'll do anything to expedite our tasks, and we end up eating everywhere: in the car, at our desk, or on the couch while watching TV. I'm sure some people snack while having sex—more "bangs" for the buck.

Exercise Is Good for You, but . . .

Over the years we've come to believe that when we eat too much, we can "burn it off" by working out at the gym or going for a fast walk or run. This mentality has given us a false sense of what's possible. It takes an extraordinary amount of exercise to balance overeating.

Once again, we tend to look at celebrities in the media—those masterpieces of chiseled muscles and toned abs—as role models, and they all obviously work out regularly to achieve their fit bodies. However, they also get to look that way because *it's their job.* It doesn't happen for them by doing the stationary bike for 20 minutes at Bally's and then following it up with a Domino's deep-dish three-cheese pizza for lunch. They have to eat as much as a mouse and exercise with the endurance of a lioness running down a wildebeest.

Very few of us are going to eat and exercise with that sort of intensity or regimen. But we have to understand that that's what it takes—in order to get buff, it takes enormous amounts of time and effort. Those who want the perfect physique of a television star are going to have to make it their full-time job. Anything short of that will require an understanding of how to balance the right amount of exercise with the right amount of caloric intake.

I highly recommend the book *The Biology of Belief* by Bruce Lipton, Ph.D. Dr. Lipton began his career as a cellular biologist and has become one of the most progressive thinkers on the quantifiable links between the mind and body. In this book, he shows how we can use our thoughts and energy to affect our bodies on the cellular level. Fascinating material!

Food Stress

The constant confusion about what to eat and how good or bad it is has created a culture that makes eating stressful. When you're always worried about what you're ingesting, it gives your body the wrong messages. Do you act like a forensic scientist when it comes to what you eat? When you continually analyze or forecast gloom and doom over every morsel, you're no longer experiencing pleasure.

On top of that comes another layer of stress, which takes the form of guilt. Not only do some people look at eating as a sinful activity, but they also relate their "transgressions" to everyone they meet. I'm so tired of these "food confessions." Why do I have to hear folks tell me how bad they feel over having some ice cream? Perhaps there should be a Church for Food Sinners, with weekly sermons on the horrors of snacks from hell. Maybe a carton of Häagen-Dazs could be sacrificed. You could step into the confession booth to admit to a handful of potato chips and be told to substitute soy crisps as your penance.

The interesting sidebar to this is that there's scientific evidence to support the fact that our cells communicate with each other. It may very well be that the more we tell ourselves that everything we eat makes us fat or sick, the more likely it is that we'll actually *become* fatter and sicker.

In Michael Pollan's book *In Defense of Food: An Eater's Manifesto,* he notes that psychologists have recently suggested that the DSM-IV (the *Diagnostic and Statistical Manual of Mental Disorders,* published by the American Psychiatric Association) needs to recognize a new eating disorder that they're seeing in more and more patients: orthorexia nervosa, which is simply "an unhealthy obsession with healthy eating." Dr. Steven Bratman, who coined the term in 1997, considers the disorder to be a problem when food becomes a source not just of nutrition, but of virtue and self-esteem—that is, when eating "bad foods" implies that one is a bad person, and doing so causes guilt and self-loathing. Bratman has written a book called *Health Food Junkies: Orthorexia Nervosa: Overcoming the Obsession with Healthful Eating.* In it, he outlines the following ten symptoms of orthorexia nervosa. Do you recognize any of these traits in yourself or your loved ones?

1. Spending more than three hours a day thinking about healthy food

2. Planning your day's menu more than 24 hours ahead of time

3. Taking more pleasure from the "virtuous" aspect of food than from actually eating it

4. Finding your quality of life decreasing as the quality of your food increases

5. Becoming increasingly rigid and self-critical about your eating

6. Basing your self-esteem on eating healthy foods and having a lower opinion of people who do not

7. Eating "correct" foods to the avoidance of all that you've always enjoyed

8. Limiting the time you spend with friends and family because you can only eat properly at home

9. Feeling guilt or self-loathing when you eat "incorrect" foods

10. Deriving a sense of self-control from eating properly

The Food Police

The latest attempt to restore sanity to the ever-expanding girth of the American public is the policing of its population by the government. Recently I read an article in *USA Today* about a town in Mississippi that was pushing legislation making it illegal for restaurants to serve obese patrons. I thought I was actually going to laugh my ass off, which would have been a better idea than the bill they wanted to pass. Imagine a squad of diligent individuals dressed in sweat suits and armed with tranquilizer guns, scales, and fat calipers. After all, some people appear to be thin but are overweight according to their BMI (body mass index), so how can you tell unless you test them? And what do you do with these folks after you arrest them? Perhaps a week in jail with just bread and water? Or maybe they could walk through town wearing a sandwich board that says: "I'm fat and I can't stop eating." This is all about shaming people, right?

California just passed a law banning trans fats from all restaurants. If you're caught with the goods, you get fined $10,000. I realize the value in protecting the general population, but where does it end? We live in a society that believes so much in freedom that we don't outlaw guns that are used to commit murder, yet we think we should be able to stop people from eating a doughnut. *Isn't that ridiculous!*

Why don't we spend equal amounts of time and money creating bills that educate us on ways to create healthier lifestyles? It's completely idiotic that we've eliminated recess, phys ed, home ec, and other such classes from our schools; and at the same time, we're spending money passing unenforceable laws to police what people eat . . . duh!

Faux Foods

I'm continually astounded by the number of foods whose natural ingredients have been substituted with artificial ones that simulate the originals. Sugar substitutes were designed to help diabetics, but then they suddenly took on a life of their own, and now most people use them as a means to save calories. How much sense does it make to ingest a substance that lowers caloric value if it might end up damaging your health? I'd rather have a teaspoon of sugar (18 calories) than ingest a substance that has to be tested on rats.

According to an article published in July 2008 by *Parade Magazine:* "New research suggests that even noncaloric sugar substitutes, whether 'natural' or artificial, may contribute to weight gain. Researchers at Purdue University published a study in February showing that rats gained weight when fed foods artificially sweetened with saccharin." These findings support an earlier study of more than 18,000 people, which found an increased risk in weight gain by drinking one diet soft drink a day. The other significant finding is the possibility that artificial sweeteners can alter metabolism. A can of Coke has 39 grams of sugar, along with caramel coloring, phosphoric acid, and caffeine. Diet Coke, which is touted as sugar free, has about 20 additional ingredients that all sound as if they were created by a paint factory.

I'm not advocating the drinking of soft drinks at all, but I find it ironic that people will often choose a fatty meal or a hot-fudge sundae and couple it with a diet soda. I believe that many of these folks have deluded themselves into believing that it somehow balances their overeating. As if in making a "virtuous" choice of a zero-calorie drink, they prove that they're *trying* to lose weight, regardless of what else they may be doing.

Over the last 20 years or so, a whole host of products have been created that are supposed to satisfy our cravings for fats, sweets, and carbohydrates with lower amounts of whatever it is we want to avoid. The "Lite" craze! It has also mesmerized us into believing that we're eating "diet food," so many of us eat twice as much of the fake stuff. And often upon close examination, we find that they have virtually as many calories as the real thing. In fact, in order to preserve taste, low-fat versions often have more sugar, and sugar-free versions may have more fat or higher amounts of an alternative sweetener. Voilà—one of the reasons for the obesity epidemic.

Watch the halo effect! A paper in the *Journal of Consumer Research* tells of a study in which people were questioned about how many calories they consumed by eating at McDonald's versus Subway. Keep in mind, of course, that the latter very aggressively markets itself as a healthy choice. When given meals of equal calorie content, the Subway diners on average believed that they were eating significantly fewer calories than the McDonald's eaters. And on top of that, McDonald's customers tended to order a diet drink, conscious of the high calorie counts of their sandwiches. On the other hand, Subway customers ordered full-sugar soft drinks and often dessert.

Be wary of faux or artificial foods. "Faking" can manifest itself in many areas of our lives (as women well know!). Let's now take a look at how we try to disguise our weight gain by rearranging the truth.

CHAPTER THREE

The Truth Will Set You Free

"Honesty is the best policy—in the schoolroom and in front of the mirror."

Wouldn't it be refreshing if we could simply be honest about our weight issues? Instead, we seem to do everything possible to obscure the truth and pretend we're not overweight. My favorite piece of "truthiness" is: *I'm vertically challenged and horizontally impaired.*

I remember a time when nobody pulled any punches about what you weighed. The school I attended as a youngster had a facsimile of Nurse Ratched who diligently weighed and measured us. If you were becoming ungainly, she'd call it to your parents' attention. And since children's perception of their well-being wasn't necessarily part of her curriculum, she didn't have to worry about being taken away by the self-esteem police or if overly protective parents would have her doing hard time at Attica. She told the truth and held the parents accountable, stressing that their children's welfare was at stake. I'm sure she didn't mince words if the parents were heavy, too.

When you stepped on the scale at the doctor's office, sometimes he or she would tsk-tsk as the sliding balance kept going farther to the right. Today, you're asked if you want to see how much you weigh and actually have the option of facing the other direction so that you don't have to know. Perhaps doctors' offices ought to hand out black shrouds to place over mirrors so the delusion can be complete.

There are also clothing stores that use 1, 1.5, 2, 2.5, and so on as a way of sizing. So if we wear the 3.5, we can still think we're svelte. These retailers know that the average woman wants to feel like she can still fit into a size 4 despite the fact that the actual size fits a body that we all know is a 16. Even the mirrors in most of the stores are made to give us the illusion of being thinner—they're slanted, and it can make a big difference in how we look. Isn't it time we tried to get real with ourselves?

"Mirror, Mirror on the Wall"

I bet that everyone reading this book will relate when it comes to the most traumatic, depressing thing I've ever faced. No, it's not a bad dye job, a love gone wrong, or an unappreciative family. It's the *dressing-room mirror.*

After standing in front of many of them, I'm certain that the manufacturers of these icons of evil are the same folks who make mirrors for magicians. Have you ever noticed how devious they can be? You can look thin in one and fat in another. I love the thin mirrors . . . but then who wouldn't? I also appear taller in them, which is really terrific since I'm getting closer and closer to being a hobbit as I age. I always come out of the dressing room smiling, and the sales clerk invariably says, "That must have looked really good on you." I like to respond: "No, it didn't, but I'd love to buy the mirror!"

Have you noticed that the more expensive the clothing store is, the better you look in the mirror? The cheaper stores usually have mirrors that are sort of wavy and make you look like a figure from a Salvador Dalí painting.

Trying on bathing suits is the worst. And it's really discouraging when you've been working out ferociously, and what's being reflected back isn't what you had expected. *How could this be? These are not my arms or thighs. There has to be a mistake. An alien must have come into my bedroom and traded parts as I slept. . . .*

How about the suggestions included in many self-help books that tell you to look into the mirror and say: *I love myself just as I am?* This is supposed to be helpful when you're in one of those self-deprecating modes—for example, while trying on clothes. Lots of luck! I *don't* love myself just as I am: I want to be 5'8", with long legs, a thin waist, and long hair that I can toss over my shoulder. Aside from that, I'm okay.

Men don't seem to be bothered by mirrors. If they want to know how they look, they usually ask their significant other. They're definitely onto something. Unless your partner wants to get rid of you, most people aren't going to say, "You look like a trash compactor in that outfit."

Well, there's only one answer: I need to buy a *thin mirror* and carry it everywhere I go.

A decade ago, it was rare to find elastic waistbands in clothing except on pants made for the elderly because it's easier to take them on and off. Not anymore! Now it's common for slacks to be fitted with them so that as you increase in girth, they can grow along with you. So the clothes industry has found a way for you to ignore the fact that you shouldn't be able to fit into your pants. Big T-shirts are more in style now, too . . . not surprising, since there's so much to cover up.

In fact, styles seem to vacillate between overly big and teeny-weeny. It isn't unusual to see people walking around wearing clothing that they seem to have been shoehorned into. If you're Angelina Jolie that might work, but when your rolls of fat are starting to give birth to smaller rolls, and your blouse starts to make you look like a gigantic meatball, then it's time to get real.

> I often hear people suggest that their obesity is due to a suspected food allergy. Most of us are just allergic to too much food!

Yes, I know that everyone has the right to dress as they please, but this isn't about freedom. We also have the right to drink vodka instead of juice at breakfast, but it's not very wise. We need a reality check; and I think it's unfortunate that society is happy to help perpetuate the myth that we're not as heavy as we are. Who is that helping?

Is your clothing adding to your ability to fool yourself about your weight and the shape you're in? Do you always find yourself using the "dark top, light bottom" trick when putting together an outfit? Do you bring out the silver bullet at the sight of horizontal stripes? I'm not saying that you shouldn't choose clothes that flatter your shape, but you need to be honest with yourself if what you're doing is just trying to hide or deny what you really look like.

Another way you may find it hard to get real and face the facts is if you travel in a pack with individuals who behave in similarly unhealthy ways. When you have a groupthink going on, it helps fuel your irrational behavior. You'll realize that you tell each other how great you look at the expense of the truth because it makes everybody feel good. It perpetuates the "right" way in which the group should interact.

Research has shown that if we hang out with or are married to an overweight person, we'll start to become overweight ourselves as we move toward *their* habits. It makes perfect sense to me. Humans are pack animals; we like to do what others around us are doing. And if the people around us are always overeating, it justifies our natural instinct to give in to the desire to gorge ourselves. And as we become fatter and fatter, we all know that the old adage rings true: *Misery loves company.* If all of our friends are overweight, it's easier to feel that our experience is normal.

There are also organizations that offer support to overweight people, such as the National Association to Advance Fat Acceptance, Fat Is Beautiful, and Largesse, which calls itself "the network for size esteem." Now I'm not for a moment saying that people who are obese should be hiding under a rock someplace, but I don't think we should be kidding ourselves by thinking that there's nothing wrong with it. There *is* something wrong with obesity—everyone knows it. It has been linked to numerous chronic health problems and diseases; there's really nothing good about it.

If we truly want to become healthier, we need to be involved with someone (or a group) who feeds that inner part of us that knows what's best for us. I'm fortunate to travel with my best friend, who's invested in keeping fit and well. She's also an avid truth teller. If I were turning into an avocado with legs, I can be assured she'd say something to me. My children wouldn't hesitate either. I'm blessed with kids who know the benefits of being in good shape, and they always ask me if I'm working out, which helps me stay on course. Although the course is somewhat rocky. . . .

The Reality Check

Pull out a notebook or your journal, and answer the following questions. Be honest!

1. How often do you fudge about your weight to yourself and others?

2. How many skirts or pairs of pants do you have with elastic waistbands?

3. Do you often wear clothing that floats around you and could double as a bed-spread?

4. How many of your friends are in good shape?

5. Does your significant other work out regularly?

6. Do you know what constitutes a healthy diet and what you need to do to stay strong and fit? Does your information come from a reliable source?

7. How many of your family members are overweight? Can you see a theme through the generations?

8. Do you have any clue as to how much food you eat on a daily basis? If not, is there someone else who can help you estimate it?

It's so easy to fool ourselves about a great deal of things. What eventually happens is that we actually start to believe our own half-truths, which makes it even more difficult to change. Many of us consider ourselves "fit" if we don't pass out after walking up a flight of stairs or think that we look good in size XXXL clothing.

Randy Pausch, a professor at Carnegie Mellon University who recently died of pancreatic cancer, wrote in his bestseller *The Last Lecture* that we should always tell the truth. When we begin to acknowledge our stumbling blocks, it becomes easier to overcome them. One of the ways we can begin to assess how much we eat, where we eat, and why we eat the things we do is to start a food diary. I have to admit that I've never been too compliant with this technique; however, I'm willing to take a shot at it again based on the following information I read in an article from *Time* magazine by Sanjay Gupta, M.D.:

I started the [food] diary because I wanted to test the striking new results of a paper published in the August [2008] issue of *American Journal of Preventive Medicine*. Scientists at several clinical-research centers in the U.S. found that dieters who kept a food diary lost twice as much weight as those who didn't. . . . Victor Stevens of Kaiser Permanente Center for Health Research in Portland, Ore., told me that "hands down, the most successful weight-loss method was keeping a record of what you eat." In the six-month study, participants who kept a food journal six or seven days a week lost an average of 18 lb. compared with an average of 9 lb. lost by non-diary keepers.

Foods That Fool You into Thinking They're Healthy

- *Energy Bars.* Energy bars don't necessarily give you energy. Many of them are loaded with as many calories and as much fat as a candy bar. But some people scarf one down thinking that it's as healthy as a carrot. And believing that a three- or four-inch bar is a substitute for a meal is crazy.

- *Granola.* Most granola is high in fat, sugar, and calories. Low-fat versions often swap sugar for fat and have as many calories as the regular version.

Learning to Separate the Wheat from the Chaff

I so wish I had a talk show just so I could rant about all the insane crap that's written about health. It would probably fill the Grand Canyon. It's so pathetic to think that we're in an era that consistently exploits the general public with false promises. Never has so much been written that has so little substance about how to lose weight, exercise, and reduce stress. Why don't we have some kind of agency that speaks up about the scams that continually try to take advantage of us? It's very difficult, especially in the face of all the media and marketing, for most people to sort out fact from fiction.

All drugs have to be approved by the FDA and must pass rigorous protocols to be placed on the market. And even then, we know that some still end up being pulled off the shelves due to unexpected side effects. However, this isn't the case with vitamins, diets, exercise gadgets, or stress-reduction gimmicks—all of which are unregulated. I swear that some of the diet plans published today are totally fabricated by people who sit in their basements, giggling over what kind of nonsense they can pull off on the public: "I know . . . the eat-all-the-ice-cream-you-want-for-a-week diet! Lose weight and look ten years younger! That'll be a bestseller!"

For the last several decades, most of the snake-oil mentality around diets was directed at women, but now they're targeting men and teenagers as well. We cannot continue to be victims of this industry! However, it can only change when we see the folly inherent in the ads and articles and start asking questions that challenge the craziness.

Don't assume that just because you see people in ads wearing lab coats while selling a new diet book or pill that it's guaranteed to work. These folks may have been paid big bucks to promote the product or may have no idea what they're talking about. And everyone wears lab coats these days . . . even someone trying to sell you a mattress.

Plus, more and more we're finding out that when we see celebrities on talk shows opening up to the host about how some drug or special diet plan changed their life, they're actually being paid by the company that makes the product. Nobody tells us that these moments of "honest talk" are actually the same as watching a commercial!

Be on the lookout for some of the deceptive rhetoric and gimmicks designed to pull the wool over your eyes. Always be wary of outlandish claims or promises that seem too good to be true. Here are some examples that may sound familiar:

— *"Melt fat away."* We should all be so lucky! Fat just doesn't "melt away." When we lose weight, we lose fat, and that takes burning more calories than we consume. Cardiovascular exercise and weight training will help build muscles so that it's not lost along with the fat.

— *"Scientifically formulated for rapid weight loss."* Who are these scientists, and where are all the people who took this potion?

— *"Clinically proven."* By whom? Where were the studies done? How many were there, and how long did they go on?

— *"Lose belly fat the easy way with the new Belly-Fat Blaster."* This is so ridiculous. You cannot lose fat in one particular spot on your body. Stomach fat comes off along with all other body fat when you lose weight. You can tone the muscles underneath the rolls of stomach fat, but if you really want to see those muscles, you have to lose weight. This myth just doesn't want to die. Have you ever seen a really overweight person with a six-pack? No, you haven't, and you never will.

— *"Ten days to a slimmer body, fewer wrinkles, and thicker hair."* This kind of promise is akin to a gospel meeting where people gather together to get healed. There's no program or method that has the potential to cure everything. Once you read about something that claims that it can do just about anything—including making you taller—run for the hills.

— *Unique diets from specific regions or other countries: "The Voodoo Diet from the Banks of the Louisiana Swamps," "The Croatian Yak-Butter Diet," or "The Indian Shaman Program."* The idea is to make you believe that because it comes from some exotic place or people, it contains mysterious ingredients that have been used for centuries. If you look back in time, some of the inhabitants they dug up from these remote places didn't look so hot. Or the reason why folks in those areas are thin is because they have so little to eat. . . .

— *Shakes, shots, and smells.* Shakes that contain healthy ingredients are probably okay in a pinch, but they can't be a long-term solution. You need to chew. They aren't a viable substitute for three nutritious meals a day. Smelling lavender or peppermint or snakeskin isn't going to really help you shed pounds either. Aromatherapy can certainly be a positive factor in certain situations but only as one small element of a full, rational program of calorie awareness and exercise. And the only kind of "weight-loss shot" that works is an injection of common sense.

— *"Get slim for good."* Of course that sounds great, but only believe it when it's coupled with a way to help you become invested in your dietary intake on a daily basis and commit to a lifestyle that values movement, energy, and well-being. Otherwise, the only way you're going to be slim for life is if you die.

— *Celebrity diets.* You see the headlines in *People* or *OK!* magazine all the time: "How J.Lo, Britney, Nicole, and Tubby the Tuba lost all their weight!" Good for them, but you can't use celebrities as role models for your lifestyle. First of all, it's unlikely that what you're reading in those magazines is authentic. And it's also unlikely that celebrities' lifestyles are analogous to yours.

Imagine if all of those sorts of promises really paid off. We'd have a world full of people who were healthy, happy, and fit. However, the truth is that most of these idiotic concepts leave those who've tried them worse off than when they started. And most of us know that—it's just a sign of how desperate we are that so many of us are willing to buy into these unrealistic promises and plans.

I'm hoping that we'll wake up and stop being lured by these ridiculous claims. Otherwise, the only ones who will continue to benefit are the charlatans who sold us these lies, as they laugh all the way to the bank and retire on a lovely island somewhere . . . while we continue to struggle with our extra weight and lack of fitness.

It's only when we tap into our innate wisdom, common sense, and intelligence that we'll begin to make the right changes in our lifestyles that can help us become healthier and happier.

CHAPTER FOUR

How to Get Fit Without Having One

"Exercise is not an exorcism."

I started taking tap and ballet lessons when I was five years old, which grew into a lifelong love of movement. Over the years, I've studied jazz, modern and creative dance, yoga, Pilates, and ballroom dancing. To this day, I still feel incredibly happy whenever I get my body moving and grooving.

After my first divorce, I began a master's program in dance therapy and became totally intrigued with the belief that through dance, I could actually help people suffering from mental anguish. Unfortunately, I couldn't continue my studies because the reality of earning a living to support myself and my kids outweighed my ability to continue to pay for my schooling.

However, as with many things in life, opportunities arise from our trials and tribulations if we're awake to them. I decided to take what I'd learned and create a program called

"Dance/Energy." Then I tried to turn it into a business by squeaking out a little money from my already-tight budget and renting an Elks hall near my home. At this point in my life, I was a single mother with three children, two of whom were teenagers. I sent invitations to all my friends, acquaintances, and anyone else I thought might be interested in joining my program. On the first day, 70 people showed up, and I was in business.

At first I needed to supplement my income with other jobs like painting the interior of homes and wallpapering, but I knew that I'd discovered my passion and that it was resonating with others, as more and more people showed up to my classes. Eventually, the owner of a spa chain called and asked if I would be interested in training his staff in my methods. It created a huge conundrum for me since I was doing well at being an entrepreneur; however, the thought of having a company car and medical benefits was awfully appealing. I took the job but soon realized that I'd made the wrong decision.

The company president told me not to make my moves feel too much like dance or make it too much fun. He didn't want their clients to think they weren't getting a good workout. At the time, most people's idea of exercise was what Marines went through during basic training: jumping jacks, push-ups, endless sit-ups, and so on. If you didn't feel some kind of pain, many believed that you wouldn't see any results.

Here I was coming into a scene from *Rambo* and asking everyone to change course from jungle maneuvers to a mild version of *Flashdance.* Many of the clients and a few of the franchisees thought it was great. However, breaking through the anal-retentive thought process that was the corporate credo at that time as far as exercise was concerned wasn't easy. In fact, the belief that you need a workout routine with military rigor still holds a huge place in our culture. I can't tell you how many times I've watched people doing exercises at my gym that I know are going to cause a lot of pain and grief down the road. I should know because I've worked many of my joints to the extreme, and now I'm paying the price.

I finally converted a moderate amount of participants and was then asked to demonstrate my methods at a conference for spa owners. I created a routine using some of my favorite music by Earth, Wind & Fire and hoped for the best. The response was overwhelming—all of a sudden, my employers were treating me like a star. My high didn't last long, though, because I came to realize that I just couldn't survive in that kind of formulaic corporate environment. I was excited by the many possibilities of movement—not by staying within the confines of a singular way of thinking.

So we parted ways, and I went back to my original plan to teach in different places (churches, halls, schools, and so forth). My goal was to just do what I loved, which was to show people how to freely move their bodies to music, while laughing and having fun. Over the course of 20 years, I added yoga, meditation, and creative movement. I finally found the resources to create a wellness center, which at that time was an idea so far off in the horizon you'd have needed the Hubble telescope to see it. My center provided a huge array of movement possibilities and also offered counseling on nutrition and stress management. It became the jumping-off point for the career I have now.

I still bump into people who attended my classes, and they say it was the best fitness experience they ever had. I believe that the reason they enjoyed the process so much was because they had fun. For some reason, as we get older, the idea of movement as a way of life and keeping physically fit seems to become steeped in suffering. When we're children, we're taught a repertoire of movements. We learn to stand, sit, crouch, roll over, jump, twirl, skip, and a complex variety of those combinations. Kids love doing somersaults and cartwheels, and jumping into pools in the most amazing ways.

But as we grow out of childhood and into adulthood, most of us forget how thrilling it is to use our bodies to play. We don't experiment. We get up, walk around, and maybe occasionally run for a bus or jump to reach something on a high shelf. But we rarely do it just because it feels good. We lose the magical connection that comes with understanding the abilities of our own bodies. Most of us only use a few variations of the more than 2,000 movements that a human being is capable of. How can we relate to our bodies if the relationship we have to its parts is practically nonexistent?

For years, we believed that the mind and body were two separate entities. And for many of us, this is still true. We don't seem fully aware that our head is connected to our spinal column, as are our arms and legs. But thanks to the work of many people in the fields of science and mind-body studies, we're beginning to understand that we can increase our intellectual possibilities by moving our bodies. And even more interesting, the reverse is also true: our bodies can show us where our heads are at.

I've experienced positive mood changes after putting on some music and dancing around my house. It has lifted my spirits and energized me like no medication ever could. I've often recommended that when people need a boost, they should simply put on some fun music and take a few minutes to freely flit about like a child would. In fact, if you'd like to help get your children moving, I suggest playing a John Philip Sousa march at top volume in the house in the morning. Trust me: they'll make the school bus on time!

Corporations are always looking to increase productivity, but have any of them thought of instituting a midday dance break or of using movement around the workplace to help reduce stress (which has been proven to defuse anxiety caused by negative thoughts)? No. Instead, people wander off to get a coffee refill or a sugary snack—or spend time telling their co-workers how tired they are. Both of these will at best provide a temporary rush but do nothing to quell the stress.

I was knocked out by John Ratey's new book, *Spark: The Revolutionary New Science of Exercise and the Brain,* and strongly suggest that you pick it up. In it, Dr. Ratey looks at all the latest research and makes a very compelling case that exercise not only improves the functioning of our bodies, but also has a profound effect on our minds.

Little by little over the last several years, the fitness community became more enlightened, and nonmilitary types of exercise were first accepted and then finally embraced. Yoga came on the scene slowly and was positioned as a gentler way to get into shape, and it also promised that some of its relaxing poses would offer stress-reducing benefits. But as the years went by and more people were attracted to it, *voilà* . . .

new forms of yoga emerged that were hotter, tougher, and more in tune with a boot-camp mentality.

Then Pilates became the new darling of the fitness world and, like yoga, it has added more strenuous and complex forms. I can understand the need to increase levels of difficulty in order to raise the bar for people with a high aptitude. But how do we get those who are less than fit or of average ability to realize that there are alternatives to the programs that are just too difficult or embarrassing for them? It's crucial that we find ways to persuade individuals who are out of shape or prone to excuses to begin to embrace movement—and it's unlikely to come about through the sort of intimidation via the promotional images for these programs, which usually feature striking men and women in poses that look like they're straight out of Cirque du Soleil.

We're a culture of extremes. A large percentage of the population is watching a smaller percentage getting buffed. And the media bombards us with images of pumped- and gorgeous-looking people, so we start thinking, *I should look like that.* We watch as elite athletes capture Olympic medals and think, *I better sign up at the gym so I can look like that, too.* Or we see a model with a fantastic shape hawking some silly gadget that's supposed to target belly fat, and we buy it, hoping we'll achieve the same results even though we're more than 300 pounds. Women and men who have 6-packs, 12-packs, or any kind of "packs" aren't getting those results by lolling around doing a half hour of exercise and lifting minimum amounts of weight.

Activity	Calories Burned per 30 Minutes (on average)
Sleeping	22
Walking (leisurely, 2 mph)	85
Gardening	135
Raking Leaves	145
Walking (briskly, 4 mph)	170
Dancing	190
Bicycling (leisurely, 10 mph)	205
Tennis	238
Swimming (breaststroke)	333
Step Aerobics	340
Elliptical Cross-Trainer	393

You need to do the following in order to take control and get yourself on the path to good health:

1. Find a type of movement that brings you joy and one that you're able to sustain.

2. Be open, and allow yourself to experiment with various types of movement. In other words, *you need to change it up!* Too much of the same thing encourages injury and leads to the sort of boredom that makes it easier to give up.

3. Make sure you incorporate the right kinds of movement (and enough of it) that allow

you to be "fit to live." Your muscles adapt to your workload, so it's critical to figure out what type of conditioning your lifestyle requires. You need to do enough cardio so that you're able to walk up a flight of stairs without needing hits off a tank of oxygen. Strength training is necessary to prevent osteoporosis and to build endurance to get through the day, but you don't have to go crazy and try to lift a small building. Your muscles should be strong enough to carry groceries, lift young children if you have any, and keep you looking erect and youthful.

4. Discover the rush of feeling good from moving. Rid yourself of old messages and metaphors that keep you from doing what the human body was designed to do—which is to be in motion.

Have you recently said anything that sounds like the following statements?

- "I'm too tired to move after a day at work."

- "I have too much to do to find the time to take a walk."

- "I don't like exercising!"

- "It's so boring."

- "It's hard to find a place to walk."

- "I have no one to exercise with."

- "I look too fat when I move."

- "I'm too old to start anything new."

- "It's too much work."

- "When I have more time, I'll start exercising."

Often when people use these sorts of excuses over and over, they become a way of life. We become habituated to a certain way of thinking about ourselves because we've done it for so long, and it's what makes us comfortable. Changing our minds isn't easy, and it's particularly difficult when it involves moving our bodies. It takes effort and can be daunting to those who don't see themselves as the type of people who enjoy physical activity.

It doesn't take a rocket scientist to realize that our society is creating more and more lazy, inactive people. It always makes me crazy when these individuals describe themselves humorously as "couch potatoes," as if that's an acceptable lifestyle. Want a visual picture? Put a big baking potato on your couch and stare at it for a while . . . is that what you really want to aspire to?

Consider the following from the July/August 2008 issue of *Health* magazine:

> New research in *Medicine and Science in Sports and Exercise* may help explain why Americans are getting chunkier—and coax you to get off the couch. In spite of the

oft-repeated recommendation to get 30 minutes of moderate exercise (like walking) five days a week, more than 75 percent of Americans don't, according to a new study. And almost no one follows the alternative recommendation —20 minutes of "vigorous" exercise three days a week (like Spinning or kickboxing). The fact is, it's a challenge to exercise if the gym's not your thing, study author Jesse Metzger says. The best thing for you? Find something you enjoy—even a pickup game of tennis—and do it often.

In his book *Spark,* John Ratey, M.D., writes about the evidence that now points to the fact that with intense types of interval-training exercises, the pituitary gland in the brain releases human growth hormone (HGH), which "burns fat, helps layer on muscle fiber, and pumps up brain volume," according to the author. Dr. Ratey also points out: "Researchers believe that increased levels of HGH can reverse the loss of brain volume that naturally occurs as you age." So put a reminder on your door to get moving . . . before you forget that you can!

Finding Your Inner and Outer Movement

I'm going to start with what's nearest and dearest to my heart, which is moving to music. I think that everyone is born with an inner beat; you just have to find it. I imagine that you already know what makes your toes tap and body sway. Of course, simply putting on some music and moving around to it for a few minutes doesn't fill the bill for a cardiovascular workout. But you have to start somewhere, and a few minutes could lead to more and more.

If this sounds like something you might be interested in, give it a shot. I like to work out first thing in the morning because it gets me going. You might prefer afternoons or early evenings. It really doesn't matter. The exciting thing about being at home with your music is that you can do it anytime. Find a favorite song or album with a beat that makes you want to wiggle your hips. Put it on, and just start to move. Get silly: the more you move, the more benefits you'll reap. So if it feels like fun to you, fling your arms from side to side, kick your legs as high as you like, and twist your torso. Or just gently sway at first. Do whatever feels good to you, as long as you don't hurt yourself.

The significant factor in this is that when you find something that feels enjoyable, you're more likely to continue doing it. Don't worry if it's not a sweat-inducing session at first—you'll work up to that. I'm of the opinion that if you don't feel the sensation of movement with some energy and excitement in your soul, you won't be encouraged to stick with it. It's kind of like having sex for 20 years and never having an orgasm . . . it loses something in the translation.

And there are some other great reasons to incorporate music into your movement plan. Consider these amazing findings:

— *Music as medicine:* "Antidepressants and talk therapy aren't the only useful treatments for depression. A little R.E.M. or Madonna might bring relief, too. A new research review found that music therapy, listening to music in groups, exercising and singing improvised songs helped depressed people feel better." (*Health* magazine, July/August 2008)

— *"Tantilizing tango"*: "In a study published in December 2007, Gammon M. Earhart and Madeleine E. Hackney of the Washington University School of Medicine in St. Louis found that tango dancing improved mobility in patients with Parkinson's disease. . . . The researchers found that after 20 tango classes, study subjects 'froze' less often. Compared with subjects who attended an exercise class instead, the tango dancers also had better balance and higher scores on the Get-Up and Go test, which identifies those at risk for falling." (*Scientific American,* July 2008)

— *"Ballet for better balance"*: "Roger W. Simmons of San Diego State University has found that, when thrown off balance, classically trained ballet dancers right themselves far more quickly than untrained subjects, thanks to a significantly faster response to the disturbance by nerves and muscles. As the brain learns to dance, it also apparently learns to update feedback from the body to the brain more quickly." (*Scientific American,* July 2008)

One of the most interesting links between exercise and music is that it creates a "flow" state. Flow is an altered state of awareness during physical activity in which the mind and body function on "autopilot" with minimal conscious effort. Some coaches refer to this as being "in the zone." It's a state of mind not unlike being in a trance.

Much of the work in flow can be attributed to psychology professor Mihaly Csikszentmihalyi, who is noted for his groundbreaking work in the areas of creativity and happiness. He associated it with an optimal psychological state and says that it represents complete enjoyment of, and immersion in, physical activity. For many people, and I'm certainly among them, music may very well have a considerable effect on enjoyment levels during exercise.

Selecting the right music may be a key factor in keeping you entertained and helping you stick with a movement routine. And while one's music preference is highly personal, I'm going to recommend some specific songs and explain how they resonate with your physiology.

The human heartbeat is particularly attuned to sound and music. Your heart works in concert with the beat, so choosing the right rhythms can enhance, or detract, from your workout. You'd think that the music played in many health clubs would reflect that, but a lot of it reminds me of the sound track from a horror film.

It seems that even with all of the innovations in fitness equipment, little has been done to seriously examine the role that music could play in making working out even more effective. Our heart rate responds to the variables of tempo and volume. A great deal of research has been done to show how meditation and music work hand in hand. I doubt that it's possible to relax the mind and body with heavy-metal music, but I'm sure there are some who would disagree.

I know this probably sounds simplistic, but it's true nonetheless: *The faster the music, the faster the heart will beat; the slower the music, the slower the beat.* A lower heartbeat will quiet respiration, calming the mind and easing physical tension. What many people don't realize is that hard-driving rock music may be energizing, but according to researchers, it lowers the quality of your workout. Music can also affect blood pressure—excessive noise has been shown to increase it by 10 percent. In a world so inundated with noise pollution, it makes perfect sense to try to listen to songs that are better suited for your blood vessels.

Two of the most exciting effects that music has on working out are the release of endorphins, which are chemical cousins to opiates such as heroin and morphine, and the ability to increase immune function. The natural high one feels from listening to great songs while working out is an unbeatable combination. And the elevation of T cells (lymphocytes that boost immunity to disease) should be an amazing incentive to stay motivated.

When I taught exercise classes, I'd sprinkle in some humorous observations along with my instruction. Laughing is also an aerobic activity. As Norman Cousins, the author of *Anatomy of an Illness* and a trailblazer in the healing power of humor, once said, "Laughter is inner jogging." In fact, you can burn up to 40 calories when you laugh for ten minutes. Sounds like a great plan!

Of course, it's difficult to lift a weight and laugh at the same time, but you can certainly add laughter to your cardio workouts by listening to your favorite stand-up comedians in lieu of music or by finding instructors who don't take themselves too seriously.

The following are some average heartbeat rates achieved during different stages of a workout, paired with some of my suggested song choices:

70–90 Beats per Minute
(Warm-Up)

- "Sweet Love," Anita Baker
- "Shiver," Maroon 5
- "Hands Up," The Black Eyed Peas
- "Minister of Rock 'n Roll," Lenny Kravitz

90–120 Beats per Minute
(Weight Lifting, Rowing, Slow Walking, Hiking)

- "Superstition," Stevie Wonder
- "Wannabe," Spice Girls
- "I Want You Back," *N Sync
- "Walking on Broken Glass," Annie Lennox

120–135 Beats per Minute
(Power Walking, Hiking, Treadmill, Step Aerobics, Interval Training)

- "Proud Mary," Creedence Clearwater Revival
- "Light My Fire," The Doors
- "Dance to the Music," Sly & the Family Stone
- "Opposites Attract," Paula Abdul
- "Go West," Pet Shop Boys

135+ Beats per Minute
(Jogging, Bicycling, Aerobics)

- "Beat It," Michael Jackson
- "Take It Easy," Eagles
- "Out in the Cold," Tom Petty and the Heartbreakers
- "Rehab," Amy Winehouse
- "Radio Nowhere," Bruce Springsteen
- "Sleep Through the Static," Jack Johnson

Make It Fun

Women are obsessed with their butts and thighs. When I taught fitness, I'd hear a constant outpouring of "My thighs are too fat!" or "My butt needs to be higher!" (I've rarely, if ever, heard a man utter these words.) At that period in my life, I was equally obsessed and often came up with difficult exercises to pinpoint these areas. One of my favorites was having everyone lie on their backs with their legs wide apart, and then they'd proceed to do 50 or more butt-lifting repetitions in various ways to feel "the burn." In order to keep everyone going, I told them to visualize the Blue Angels overhead doing a spectacular aerobatics show just for them. I also told them to imagine themselves having seductive messages written on the inside of their thighs. It usually made everyone crack up, which of course pumped them up and allowed them to go longer than they thought possible.

Many fitness instructors would help their members tremendously if they lightened up and added the element of laughter to their classes. Instead, the routines are often done with such seriousness that you'd think they were in training to protect their village from attack. Getting in shape shouldn't be a forced march.

If there's an elixir like the fountain of youth, it's exercise. Do it with a spirit of fun, and you'll find yourself falling in love with moving your body and craving more. Visualize yourself as that little boy or girl who never wanted to stop playing. Move throughout the day just to feel free and whimsical. You don't need the right setting to make a game out of walking down the street. Walk fast and then slow; turn around and walk backward, if you dare. Take a jump rope to work and find a place where you can jump for a few minutes. Hop on one leg, then another, twirl, skip, and jump from side to side.

It's too bad that we're so afraid to look foolish. I wonder how many of us would last if we were in a group of three-year-olds for a day and had to imitate their movements. Perhaps that's one of the reasons we're less and less fit with age—we become so conservative with our movements. We don't use it, so we lose it!

Wii Fit

I've tried the Wii Fit (the new video game for fitness) and can tell you that it's enormous fun for people of all ages. I have friends in their 60s who do it with their grandchildren.

It does take a bit of an investment: you need to buy the Wii video-game machine and the separate balance board, and then hook it all up to your TV. But if it will keep you moving, it's well worth it!

The balance board is a small platform that you step onto. When you start, it actually calculates your measurements, including your weight and BMI. And then you create a little character that represents you, which shows up on your TV screen.

There are all sorts of fitness exercises and games that you can play on the board; and videos guide you through every step. You can try simple toning exercises; play balancing games such as slalom skiing, where you lean from side to side as if you were guiding yourself through the flags (maintaining good balance and posture really benefits people as they age); and even learn simple yoga poses, as it shows how you're doing by monitoring whether you're keeping your center of balance steady. You can also practice aerobic activities, including a beginning step class or jogging in place.

The program keeps a running record of how often you work out and how you're progressing. It also tracks your skill level for each game you engage in as well as your weight and BMI.

The Wii Fit is fun and easy to use—and has dozens of options for beginners and more serious fitness buffs to keep you entertained.

One of the greatest motivators I've found to keep myself moving is a pedometer. I put it on first thing in the morning and use it to monitor how active I am on a daily basis. The ultimate goal is to do 10,000 steps a day to achieve a healthy amount of physical activity, which is close to 60 minutes of exercise. The concept began as a Japanese fad known as "manpo-kei," which means "10,000 step meters" in Japanese, and now it's even being pushed by the renowned Cooper Clinic in Dallas.

Once you have your pedometer, take about a week to figure out the average number of steps you take in an ordinary day. Many individuals who are overweight take approximately 2,000 to 3,000 steps a day, which is practically an invalid level. The fun of competing against yourself can really be a motivator, and I find that it pumps me up. I'll sometimes just walk back and forth in my kitchen while I'm on the phone, which helps ratchet up the number of steps I'm going to accumulate for that day.

Choosing a program that fits your lifestyle and activates a passion for movement is highly individual. I believe it also can change and progress if you're aware of when you've simply hit the wall with your choice. The beauty of a pedometer is that you can look at it periodically and decide to ramp it up. The more you walk, the more fit you'll become.

We're so used to our sedentary lifestyle in America that we drive around in our cars for ten minutes looking for a parking spot close to a store entrance; instead, we could have parked a block away, gotten some exercise, and even saved time. I predict that if we continue our slothful ways, we'll have to develop some kind of robot to carry us around because we'll look like pods who have little stumps for legs.

How to Step It Up

Here are some ways to increase your steps when you have your pedometer on:

- Walk around your house whenever a commercial comes on (if you're watching TV).

- Walk while you're talking on your cordless phone or cell phone.

- Be creative when you can't go outside—no excuses for bad weather, unless you live in the tundra. Go to the mall and walk there. Take a buddy.

- Make a game out of it. If you're walking in nature, think of things like no stopping until you see five squirrels; if you're in a city, how about you keep walking until you spot seven Volvo station wagons?

- Park far away. Have fun with it. Tell your kids to find the farthest spot in the parking lot so they can also get the exercise they need.

- Give your kids their own pedometers as well. Make it a family game to see who's racking up the most steps each day and create a fun reward. Childhood obesity is becoming an epidemic, and it's a horrible legacy we're leaving our children with. We're not demonstrating what a healthy life should be. Researchers are saying that this is the first generation that won't live longer than the one before it, mainly due to poor lifestyle habits. It all begins with us!

The best way to track your progress is to use an activity log. Some people are really good at journaling and maintaining records, and if you're one of them, then I highly recommend that you keep this kind of running statement of how much you move each day and in what ways. I have to admit that although I know that those who diligently monitor their food intake and activities do better at compliance, I'm not great at it myself. I always start out strong, but after about a week, I get sick of it and don't follow through.

We must be realistic and come to grips with what we will and won't do consistently. I realize that I'm not good at journaling, but that's okay with me because I know that I keep up my daily routine without it. I'm not bored by exercising; I'm bored by journaling! If it was the other way around, I hope I'd see the sense in persuading myself to write.

If you try too hard to do it all, you'll invariably fail. When I owned my wellness center, women would often tell me that they were going on vacation in a few weeks and needed to tone their arms, legs, and abdomens . . . and lose 15 pounds. This can only fall into the category of *ridiculous*. What could that sort of goal lead to but frustration? The few weeks would pass, and even if my clients tried their best, they couldn't achieve what they were hoping for and ended up feeling defeated.

The drive toward fitness has to be long term and consistent. However, if there's one thing you take away from this chapter, know that it's much better to start small than not to start at all. For example, without much effort, you can simply practice visualizing yourself doing an activity like walking, jogging, or strength training. Although I don't recommend this as an ongoing way to stay fit, it has some great possibilities. Scientists have seen gains in performance levels from athletes who also practice their skills in their mind.

This might be a fun thing to try before you go to sleep instead of worrying about something that might or might not happen tomorrow (like so many of us do). See yourself looking fit and trim walking down the street—your head is held high, and you have a great attitude. Or go one step further: picture yourself bicycling down a country road, swimming in a cool lake, or participating in a sport that you used to enjoy. You may notice some positive shifts in your attitude and behavior, but once again, visualization doesn't take the place of physical activity. Nothing happens in a vacuum (unless you're a piece of dirt).

Five Mistakes That Sabotage Your Exercise Routine

1. *Comparing yourself to others who are younger, thinner, and more buffed.* Yeah, those folks at your gym look great. Just remember that no matter what they're doing, they're going to die anyway—they'll just have a smaller coffin. But this isn't about them; it's about *you.* "Be the change you wish to see in the world," as Gandhi said.

2. *Falling for advertisements that say you can easily develop firmer muscles; longer, leaner legs; higher, fuller breasts; or any*

other bullshit! Everyone has developed or inherited a certain body type and attitude. Physiology is a huge factor in how or what you can do with your figure. Can you improve yourself? Of course you can. Can you make the most of what you've got? Yes! If you're short and squat, is all the exercise in the world going to magically turn you into Gisele Bündchen? I wish!

3. *Blindly believing when someone tells you about how they lost 12 inches from their waist doing the new pole-dancing routine they saw on Jerry Springer.* Please! Why not take exercise classes from a trained monkey? That might work, too.

4. *Buying stupid gadgets or creams that profess to eliminate cellulite.* They don't work. Cellulite is primarily a female issue, and there's no evidence to support that it comes from toxins, floxins, or a bout of malaria. Let's get real! That's just more bullshit. Exercise may help, as well as stress reduction, a nutritious diet, and massage.

5. *Trusting "experts" who have no real credibility in the field.* It makes much more sense to believe someone like Miriam Nelson who runs the exercise physiology lab at Tufts and has written several books on health and fitness than some bimbo who's modeling a bikini in an ad for thermogenic supplements that supposedly burn fat. *Oy vey!*

If You're Ready for the Next Step

If you're really committed, find a qualified fitness professional who can assess your fitness level and offer you guidance. Make sure that you choose someone who's certified by a credible organization like the American College of Sports Medicine. You'll need to do a little research and trust your instincts. But be cautious: there are less reputable clubs and trainers out there making all kinds of claims and seemingly have no concept of how human anatomy works.

You should look for someone who obviously can see what your individual needs are and has specific ideas on ways to work with the current state of your muscles and joints. If you're really out of shape and your trainer insists you start off with 50 jumping jacks, get the hell out of there.

A professional assessment should test the following areas:

- Flexibility (sit-and-reach test)
- Upper-body strength
- Lower-body strength
- Abdominal strength
- Cardio fitness

Most reputable gyms give clients a "sub-max test," which evaluates your heart rate when you're working at less than your maximum effort. However, you must go to a physician for a "maximal test," in which you go to about 75 to 85 percent of your maximum heart rate. This will give you the most accurate picture of your heart's efficiency.

You should also have your BMI (body mass index) measured. Most people still just rely on a scale to determine their level of fitness, and although it's a good idea to weigh yourself, the real benchmark for measuring body fat is through your BMI. If you're interested in knowing your individual BMI, the Centers for Disease Control and Prevention offers a BMI calculator on their Website: **www.cdc.gov/nccdphp/dnpa/ healthyweight/assessing/bmi/index.htm**. I know just typing this in is exhausting, but it's worth it. Just enter your height and weight, and then click on the *calculate* button.

If you're okay with math, you can also easily calculate your BMI using the following simple formula:

1. Figure out your height in inches (for example, 5'3" equals 63 inches).

2. Take that number and square it. In other words, multiply your height in inches by itself (for example, 63 x 63 = 3,969).

3. Divide your weight in pounds by your height squared (120 pounds/3,969). Then multiply that number by 703.

So the BMI total for someone who is 5'3" (63 inches) and weighs 120 pounds is 21.3, which is a "normal" rating. Here are the standard weight-status categories associated with BMI ranges for adults, according to the CDC:

BMI	Weight Status
Below 18.5	Underweight
18.5–24.9	Normal
25.0–29.9	Overweight
30.0 and above	Obese

Many doctors and fitness experts state that the best way to measure body fat is not through BMI at all, but by conducting a "lean body analysis" with either a water-displacement test or with calipers. Because some people have more muscle mass than others, and muscle weighs more than fat, the BMI formulas are nothing more than an approximation.

You can also get a sense of the fitness of your body composition by calculating your waist-to-hip ratio. Use a measuring tape, and measure the circumference of your hips at the widest part of your butt, and then measure your waist at the smallest circumference, just above the navel. Divide your waist measurement by your hip measurement. A score of 1.0 or greater for men and women is a high-risk category. A waist-to-hip ratio of 0.7 or lower for women and 0.9 or lower for men indicates a low-risk category for health problems.

Your Blood Pressure

Have your health professional check your blood pressure. Home versions are often inaccurate. Ideally, it should be

115/75, which is the new standard. If it's higher than 140/90, you're considered hypertensive. Changing your habits in the ways discussed in this book could make a significant difference in your health.

"I gotta work out. I keep saying it all the time. I keep saying I gotta start working out. It's been about two months since I've worked out. And I just don't have the time. Which, uh . . . is odd. Because I have the time to go out to dinner. And uh . . . watch TV. And get a bone density test. And uh . . . try to figure out what my phone number spells in words."

— Ellen DeGeneres

There are countless reasons why it's smart to have your body tested and checked in all of these ways on the road to achieving better health, as well as losing weight. But it's also a great motivational tool: the best way to stay pumped is to have a starting point so that you can see where you began and how much you're progressing.

I hope this chapter has given you some ideas about how to keep your enthusiasm revved up when you exercise; that's the only way most people can stay committed to their goals. Similarly, you have to be passionate about eating nutritious meals. Don't be afraid to try something new. Only rabbits stay happy on a diet of lettuce. That said, let's talk about some delicious foods that will satisfy your cravings and help keep you healthy and fit. . . .

CHAPTER FIVE

Tickle Your Tongue

"If it doesn't taste good, don't eat it!"

I have to admit that I'm a "tasteaholic." It's very difficult for me to decide what I want to order at a restaurant because I want to try everything. The combinations of flavors available today are astounding and have just compounded my ability for bliss! I thought what I grew up eating was amazing, but the fact that we now have access to a global tastefest makes me insane with joy.

Have you ever wondered why foods taste so different from one another? You have about 10,000 tiny taste buds on your tongue and the roof of your mouth that act like text messages telling your brain what flavors you're sampling. Women have more taste buds than men, but insects have the most highly evolved ones. Who would have thought that a bug would be able to enjoy flavors better than I can? I'm jealous!

As you grow older, your taste buds become less sensitive (darn it!), and you find yourself more likely to eat foods or seasonings that you found too strong as a child. I notice that I've been using more pepper and hot sauces than I ever did before. There are five primary tastes: salty, sweet, sour, bitter, and umami. *Umami* is newly recognized and most clearly described as the "savory" taste sensation that's associated with meats, cheeses, and other protein-rich foods. Some researchers also believe that there should be a separate category for the taste of fat, but there's no agreement on that.

Your taste buds are the product of your genes, personal experiences, and how you've been socialized. I always think it's unfortunate for people who were brought up in families that stuck to very limited eating patterns. Ilene Bernstein, Ph.D., a professor of psychology at the University of Washington, says that everyone has at least a little bit of a sweet tooth. That's why it's so difficult to remove dessert and other tasty treats from your diet.

I came across one of Dr. Bernstein's studies several years ago, and I found it fascinating. Her research indicated a correlation between our cravings for salt and the severity with which our mothers suffered morning sickness during pregnancy. Bernstein (who co-authored the study, which was published in the journal *Appetite*) contended that researchers found that the loss of electrolytes and sodium during a woman's morning sickness has an impact on her offspring's salt preference. Amazing!

Flavor and taste seem like separate senses, but we know that's not the case when we have a cold. There's an old kid's joke that illustrates this: When does a strawberry taste like an onion? When you hold your nose!

If we've been gifted with such an amazing array of taste sensors, why in God's name do we think it's a good idea to go on diets that are very restrictive or include only bland ingredients? Shouldn't we consider that trying to take away the flavors we've grown up with and associated with comfort or fun is in direct opposition to what we desire as an outcome?

It's like me telling you not to think of an elephant for the next five minutes. You know that within seconds, no matter what else you think about, that big gray trunk is going to be swinging around inside your head.

The mind is insidious—it loves to torture you, which is why using rhetoric that makes certain foods sound toxic, repulsive, or off-limits is ridiculous. If you grew up having bacon and eggs for breakfast or enjoying ice cream for dessert, letting go of this ritual will be difficult because it was part of your upbringing. For me, the equivalent would be saying that I can't eat pasta anymore. It just doesn't work! You might as well try to convince yourself that the people you find sexy have now become ugly, or that the music you've always loved is really just noise. *What you love is what you love. . . .*

Trying to deny yourself the things that comfort you would put your taste buds into open revolt, and they'd make you salivate every time someone talked about a forbidden food. Should you just relent and eat what you want every day? Absolutely not, because you won't be providing your body with the variety of nutrients it needs—and that may well be part of the reason why your body doesn't look the way you'd like it to. But you don't have to totally eliminate your favorite foods either.

A study conducted in the 1970s attempted to determine whether there was a connection between nutrition absorption and how much a person enjoyed what he or she was eating. The researchers' findings were astounding.

Two groups of women were fed a spicy Thai meal: one group was made up of Thai women and the other was Swiss. The Thai women (to whom the food was enjoyable and familiar) absorbed 50 percent *more* iron from the meal than the Swedish women did. Then researchers served them the same meal again but first mashed it up into an unappealing paste. This time, the Thai women absorbed 70 percent *less* iron than they did when the dish looked appetizing.

The researchers concluded that eating things that are unfamiliar or unappealing are less nutritious to people than what looks and smells good to them.

We need to start considering our individual taste needs. It would also be wise to teach kids the importance of having an open mind. Whenever I take my grandchildren out to eat, I always encourage them to try something new. They initially balk, but I'm relentless. They'll say something like, "I don't think I'm going to like that," and insist on the usual kids' choice of pizza or macaroni and cheese. I always ask if they've ever tried it, and of course they say no. Then I hit them with my favorite retort: "Well, if you've never eaten it, you have no basis for making a decision on whether you like it or not!"

But don't we all know some otherwise reasonable adults who go through their entire lives acting the same way about so many things? Why don't we all open ourselves up to the infinite number of tastes and flavors that are there for the taking? Who knows—it just might be the greatest asset we have as we strive to attain a healthy weight.

Going on a program that creates a linear palate is bound to fail. No one can continue eating the same foods over and over, or those that are prepared in the exact same manner. Sure, steamed chicken is low in calories, but why not just chew on a rubber tire? I'm sure sautéing vegetables in one of those flavored-spray oils is less fattening, but how good can a food be that comes out of an aerosol can?

Look through your cupboard—does it make you start thinking of the movie *Groundhog Day?* In other words, are you noticing that you use the same few ingredients day in, day out? Think about adding some new spices such as cilantro, chili pepper, mint, sesame seeds, or dill. One of my favorites is tarragon. How about checking out different kinds of vinegar? Have you tried any of the numerous grains available, such as barley, couscous, quinoa, or wild rice? How about nuts? Go outside the box and try throwing in some pignoli, pistachios, or pecans into a salad. And when you're buying lettuce, consider endive or radicchio rather than your usual standby.

Nuts and grains are delicious and satisfying, and also give us a sense of "crunching." If we crunch while we're eating, we help ourselves reach satiety faster. I really get crazy when people recommend liquid diets. That's fine if you have no teeth or are a breast-feeding infant—otherwise, you need to chew! Here are some of my favorite dishes. How about trying some of them out?

Watercress & Endive Salad

Mix together ¾ tsp. lemon zest, 2 Tbsp. lemon juice, 1 Tbsp. olive oil, and salt and pepper to taste. Toss with 4 cups watercress, 2 chopped hard-boiled eggs, 1 slice crumbled bacon, 1 Tbsp. chopped fresh cilantro, and ½ cup corn. Serve over endive leaves.

Servings: 4 · Calories per serving: 145

Spicy Thai Shrimp Salad

Sauté ½ of a sliced red pepper and a handful of shiitake mushrooms in 1 tsp. olive oil. In a bowl, mix 2 Tbsp. lime juice, 1 Tbsp. olive oil, 2 tsp. brown sugar, and ½ tsp. crushed red pepper. Toss with 1 pound cooked shrimp; 1 cup thinly sliced cucumber; ¼ cup chopped fresh basil, cilantro, and/or mint; and the sautéed vegetables. Add 1 Tbsp. crushed pistachio nuts.

Servings: 4 · Calories per serving: 205

Two-Sesame Beef & Red Pepper Stir-Fry

¾ pound lean beef (or substitute a veggie burger)
½ cup reduced-sodium soy sauce
1 small dried hot chili pepper
1 clove chopped garlic
2 Tbsp. white wine
1 Tbsp. rice-wine vinegar
1 Tbsp. sugar
1 tsp. minced ginger root
1 Tbsp. sesame seeds
2 tsp. peanut oil
½ sliced red onion
1 sliced red bell pepper
2 stalks sliced celery
1 Tbsp. cornstarch, dissolved in 1 Tbsp. water
1 tsp. sesame oil

Slice the meat thinly. Combine the soy sauce, chili pepper, garlic, white wine, vinegar, sugar, ginger root, and sesame seeds in a small bowl. Pour it over the meat, and let marinate overnight or for at least an hour.

Heat the peanut oil in a skillet over high heat until very hot. Add the onion, red pepper, and celery; stir until translucent, but not yet soft. Add the meat and marinade, and stir-fry until the meat is cooked through (about 3 or 4 minutes). Add the cornstarch thickener and stir over high heat until the sauce thickens, about 1 minute. Remove the dried chili pepper. Drizzle sesame oil over all. Serve with rice.

Servings: 4 · Calories per serving: 285

Barley Risotto with Wild Mushrooms and Peas

¾ cup barley

¼ tsp. extra-virgin olive oil

¼ cup chopped yellow onion

½ cup frozen green peas

½ tsp. minced garlic

1½ cups assorted fresh mushrooms (such as white button, shiitake, portobello)

1 bay leaf

3 to 3½ cups vegetable stock, heated

½ Tbsp. chopped fresh thyme

1 tsp. chopped fresh oregano

⅛ tsp. kosher salt

Pinch of freshly ground black pepper

1 Tbsp. shredded parmigiano-reggiano cheese (optional)

Place ½ cup of the barley in a pan. Turn the heat to medium and cook until it's golden brown, 3 to 5 minutes. Remove the barley from the pan and set aside. Heat a medium saucepan over medium-high heat and add the olive oil. Add the onion and garlic. Cook until the onion has just softened, about 2 minutes. Add the mushrooms and cook for 1 minute. Stir in the toasted barley, the remaining 1/4 cup barley, and the bay leaf.

Stir ½ cup of the hot stock into the barley, and reduce the heat to a simmer. Cook, stirring constantly, until the barley has absorbed all the liquid. Continue adding ½ cup of hot stock at a time to the barley mixture, stirring until absorbed. Cook until the barley is tender, 20 to 30 minutes. Just before you think it's done, stir in the peas until cooked through. Stir in the thyme, oregano, salt, pepper, and cheese. Remove the bay leaf and serve.

Servings: about 5 · *Calories per serving:* 150

*"A daydream is a meal at which images are eaten. Some
of us are gourmets, some gourmands, and a good many
take their images precooked out of a can and swallow
them down whole, absent-mindedly and with little relish."*

— W. H. Auden

I've realized that as I've aged, I've beefed up the spices
and flavors in my recipes. My pantry is now loaded with
chilis (hot, hot, hot . . . and why not? *I'm* getting spicier!)
That should be everyone's goal—to feel fresh, spicy, hot, and
healthy!

CHAPTER SIX

How to Take
a Load Off
Your Mind

"The excess weight you're carrying may be in your head."

Who would have ever thought that stress could make us fat? For the most part, it's true. Doctors have known for many years that psychological forces were the most important ones in determining why we eat too much. Some people have physiological conditions that cause them to overeat or hold on to excess weight, but for the vast majority, weight gain can be attributed to our complex psyches.

"Emotional eating" (when we eat for reasons other than to satisfy our physical hunger) is one of the major causes of gaining weight. In addition, many of us inherit unhealthy eating habits from our parents. These are just a couple of examples; there are innumerable ways that our psychological makeups may be preventing us from controlling our weight gain.

But sometimes, it's even simpler than that. Let's face it—most of us look for comfort foods when we're stressed out. It's highly unlikely that we're going to pull out a bag of carrots or bean sprouts from the fridge when we're upset or anxious. It's called *comfort food* for a reason. So our modern, stressful lives seem to drive us more and more toward mindless eating and unhealthy snacking.

And on top of that, scientists have discovered that chronic stress makes your body produce excess amounts of the stress hormone *cortisol,* which has been shown to promote abdominal fat storage. It also ends up adding to your risk for diabetes and heart disease. What's really fascinating is that if you're under a lot of stress, you'll gain weight even if your caloric input hasn't changed. Stress seems to trigger a chemical reaction that encourages fat cells to grow and multiply.

Stress-related extra pounds tend to be stored around the belly. This is one of the most dangerous places for fat to end up, since it increases the risk of heart disease, hypertension, and diabetes. It's possible that women may be more vulnerable to stress—in their mood responses and cortisol reactivity —and therefore, more at risk for stress-induced eating and weight gain.

I can attest to the fact that women are definitely driven by their emotions and hormone changes. When I went through menopause, I couldn't fall asleep—and when I did, I'd wake up in the middle of the night and make a little snack to help soothe myself back to sleep. Unfortunately, that snack would often turn into a buffet.

I may be overstepping my boundaries here and acting like a faux scientist, but I believe that one of the biggest reasons why the obesity epidemic took hold in our culture is because our lives have become more and more complicated, stressed out, and undernurtured. And I'm certainly not alone in thinking that way. According to a recent American Psychological Association survey, a third of us are experiencing "extreme stress," and "nearly half [of Americans] believe stress is damaging their health, their relationships, and work productivity, and that it has gotten worse in the last 5 years."

I've been on both ends of the spectrum in the ways in which stress has affected my body. When my life is too busy and responsibilities overwhelm me, I gain weight. When I've been in the midst of something incredibly stressful like my divorce, or if a major health issue is affecting my family or me, I then get so overstressed that I lose weight. Perhaps someone should create a diet based on scaring the living hell out of people every time they go near the refrigerator.

I'm sure some of you have had similar reactions to life events. As I've become more aware of how my mind sabotages me and others, I've become a bit better at regulating my emotions and thus my eating behavior. However, some patterns are deeply ingrained and can be incredibly difficult to change. For example, my comfort food has always been pasta. I can remember coming home many a night from a road trip—totally frazzled from delayed flights, long days, and intense work—thinking about how good I was going to feel after a plate of pasta. Why wouldn't I think of pasta? It was one of my greatest sources of joy when I was a child. I associate it with the wonderful times I shared with my grandparents. The memories of sitting at the kitchen table in our brownstone in Brooklyn, surrounded by the smells of sauce marinating and garlic and onions sautéing, always make me feel loved and supported.

The thing is, there's nothing wrong with eating pasta or anything else if it makes you feel warm and cozy . . . as long as you're aware of the proper portions and stay sane about it. I couldn't stop at just one small cup or cup and a half. I needed to have a small trough.

Americans often skip breakfast or think that a bagel and a cup of coffee is a healthy way to start the day. *It's not*. A nutritious breakfast is your most important meal because it enhances how your brain functions. You should include some fiber, carbs, and protein. Greek yogurt would be a terrific addition. Try a breakfast of walnuts, blueberries, honey, and Greek yogurt—delicious *and* satisfying.

Could it be that it's so much harder for us to lose weight than our predecessors because we're biologically hindered by our stressful lifestyles? I've talked to many people who swear that they're counting calories and exercising like mad, yet they still aren't able to lose weight. Perhaps it's because they're simply too anxious or tense. The stress hormone known as the "corticotrophin-releasing factor" tips the body's energy balance in favor of conservation. Anxiety triggers our hereditary biological reaction to hold on to excess weight because we might be facing famine.

In fact, studies have shown that there's a link between what we eat and how we feel. Researchers studying nutrition have discovered that certain foods affect our brain chemistry:

Research by Judith Wurtman, a professor at the Massachusetts Institute of Technology (MIT), has focused on how certain foods alter one's mood by influencing the level of certain brain chemicals called neurotransmitters. While many other factors influence the level of these chemicals, such as hormones, heredity, drugs, and alcohol, three neurotransmitters—dopamine, norephinephrine, and serotonin—have been studied in relation to food, and this research has shown that neurotransmitters are produced in the brain from components of certain foods. ("Mood-Food Relationships": **www.faqs.org/nutrition/Met-Obe/ Mood-Food-Relationships.html**)

Foods such as cereal, candy, and yes, pasta—that is, sweets and refined starches—seem to produce a temporary increase in serotonin, which has a calming effect. It could very well be that a vicious cycle is put into play. The more stressed you become, the more you crave the foods that help calm you, and the result may be that you then effectively become addicted to those foods and their calming effects. In this way, certain foods may resemble what alcohol and drugs do to the brain.

You may have noticed that you feel drowsy after eating a large meal of pasta. Carbohydrates increase serotonin because they increase tryptophan in the brain, which is the amino-acid precursor of serotonin. You used to be able to buy tryptophan in health-food stores as a sleep aid until a batch of it caused paralysis in some people, and it was subsequently stopped from being sold over the counter. The only way you can get it now is through a prescription.

Protein-rich foods help stimulate norepinephrine and dopamine, and they appear to block serotonin so that they're more apt to increase alertness and concentration. Here are some foods and their possible effects on the brain:

Nutrient	Food Sources	Neurotrans- mitter	Proposed Effect
Protein	Meat, Milk, Eggs, Cheese, Fish, Beans	Dopamine, Norepineph- rine	Increased alert- ness, concentra- tion
Carbs	Grains, Fruits, Sugars	Serotonin	Increased calm- ness, relaxation
Calories	All Foods	Reduced blood flow to the brain	Decreased alert- ness and con- centration after a meal of excess calories

One of the most exciting discoveries in mood elevation was made by Candace Pert, Ph.D., the author of *Molecules of Emotion.* In her book, she writes that endorphins are the body's natural opiate-like chemicals that can produce a posi- tive state, decrease pain sensitivity, and reduce stress. Exercise releases endorphins and can be incredibly beneficial not only for stressed-out people but also for those who are suffering from depression. The effect that for years has been known as a "runner's high" is now understood to be achievable through more moderate amounts of exercise.

The following also releases endorphins in the body: laughter, acupuncture, chili peppers, massage, and yes, dark chocolate. Chocolate contains a substance that's related to endorphins called *phenylethylamine,* which may temporarily help improve your mood. Perhaps this is why women crave chocolate during PMS. This doesn't, however, give you per- mission to start devouring candy bars at will or to become an assistant to Willy Wonka. You still have to consider the amount of calories in a chocolate treat and factor that into a day of moderate eating.

These exciting discoveries can be part of our stress-survival kits. When used as a component of an entire wellness formula, they can keep our weight down and our moods up. However, if we don't address the situations that create stress, we'll continue to stuff ourselves without removing the causes that make us overeat in the first place.

Yes, exercise is an incredible catharsis for anxiety, helps tremendously in alleviating depression, increases cardiovascular health, and may boost metabolic rate; but you must also examine your lifestyle and how it affects your emotions if you truly want to create a balanced life. If overeating and unhealthy habits are covering up a life that isn't serving you, then no amount of exercise or dieting is going to change that. The biological and chemical triggers will still be there even when you lose the weight. It's essential to discover how to become resilient so that you can deal with the stressful people and events in your life with rational coping skills.

Once you learn these skills, you won't be as apt to succumb to eating three pizzas and downing a six-pack of Coke every time your husband leaves a wet towel on the bed, your boss is cranky, or one of your kids misbehaves. Once you begin to feed your brain more positive emotions, it may begin to rewire itself so that you'll be able to manage stress in a healthier way.

Let's take a closer look and examine how you feel and think:

1. How Do You Feel on a Given Day?

Do you wake up most days feeling vibrant, full of vitality, and enthusiastic for what lies ahead; lovingly connected to friends and family; excited about your work; and in sync with your co-workers? Do you feel that you have purpose and meaning in your life? Are you relaxed and happy? Or do you mostly feel depressed, grumpy, anxious, stressed out, fed up, and tired? Do you have trouble sleeping because you're constantly replaying things that bother you over and over in your head? Do you generally feel out of touch with what's going on around you or consistently ask yourself, *Is that all there is?*

Now, nothing is ever black or white. Life creates a variety of experiences, and some days may well feel like a mix of both positive and negative. But you want to make sure that you spend most of your time feeling like the first set of emotions I just described, or are at least striving toward them. The first line of defense in staying happy, healthy, and fit is to set your course on as many positive behaviors as possible so that you always have something to fall back on if you start to slip. To achieve this, I've developed a "Wellness Well." When I find myself heading into an abyss of unhealthy patterns, I dip into my well and tap into one of my skills that will help pull me out. Check out my list, and then create your own:

My Wellness Well

- Getting a massage
- Playing with my cat
- Talking to my friends on the phone in the morning

- Sipping tea while reading a great book
- Going to a bookstore
- Taking singing lessons
- Dancing around the house to my favorite music

Have a Happy Meal Without Going Out

Avoid conflict at the table! Breaking bread with your family doesn't mean doing it with a hatchet. Anger and hostility don't make for good digestion. Talk about bad habits, bad grades, or bad breath someplace else.

Start a ritual like the ones I remember. On Sundays, we stayed at the table almost all day. We cooked together, played games, and had vital conversations. Get everyone involved and have fun.

Make sure your meals create fond memories. There's nothing like getting older and having these great times stored in your memory bank. Don't make a big deal out of having to prepare the perfect meal. If you don't always have the time to cook, then get takeout. The most important ingredient is the time spent together. (Just remember that some takeout foods are artery cloggers, and I'm sure you know which ones they are—enough said.)

2. Are You Experiencing Major Life Changes?

Have you experienced any recent life changes that have affected your mood? There can be some very specific reasons behind your state of mind and why you may turn to food as a source of comfort.

Not only do we live in a world in which our day-to-day lives are wildly overcomplicated, but we're also often trying to manage overwhelming personal situations. Many of us aren't aware of how much these situations can impact our body and mind.

Drs. Thomas H. Holmes and Richard H. Rahe developed the Social Readjustment Rating Scale (SRRS) in the late 1960s as a way to determine whether stressful events make us more likely to contract illnesses. The SRRS demonstrated a positive correlation between how much tension people experience within a year and their increased chances of becoming ill (including experiencing depression). The following is a list of anxiety-inducing events from highest to lowest, as compiled by Holmes and Rahe.

You may be surprised to note that *positive* experiences impact your stress load as well as those that are negative.

Life Event	Life Change Unit (LCU)
Death of spouse	100
Divorce	73
Marital separation	65
Jail term	63
Death of a close family member	63
Personal injury or illness	53
Getting married	50
Being fired from a job	47
Reconciliation with spouse	45
Retirement	45
Change in health of family member	44
Pregnancy	40
Sexual difficulties	39
Addition of family member	39
Major business readjustment	39
Major change in financial state	38
Death of a close friend	37
Changing to a different line of work	36
Change in frequency of arguments with spouse	35
Mortgage for a loan or a major purchase over $100,000	31
Foreclosure on a mortgage or loan	30
Major change in responsibilities at work	29
Children leaving home	29
Trouble with in-laws	29
Outstanding personal achievement	28
Spouse begins or stops work	26

Life Event	Life Change Unit (LCU)
Starting or ending school	26
Change in living conditions	25
Revision in personal habits	24
Trouble with boss	23
Change in work hours/conditions	20
Change in main residence	20
Change in school	20
Change in recreational activities	19
Change in church activities	19
Change in social activities	18
Mortgage or loan under $100,000	17
Change in sleeping habits	16
Change in number of family gatherings	15
Change in eating habits	15
Holiday	13
Christmas	12
Minor violation of the law	11

How many of the events listed have you encountered over the past 12 months? Identify them and then add up their corresponding Life Change Units. This is what Dr. Holmes and Dr. Rahe predict:

- *Total LCU below 150:* You have a 35 percent chance of illness or accident within the next two years.

- *Total LCU between 150 and 300:* Your chance increases to 51 percent.

- *Total LCU over 300:* Your chance increases to 80 percent.

In addition, look seriously at the following issues, and think about how they may be contributing to the amount of stress you feel on a daily basis: how much you work versus how much you play; how much unpleasant or distracting noise is inflicted on you on a regular basis; how much you get touched; how often you have sex; how much interaction you have with friends and family; and how often you laugh. Also think about how seduced you've been by new technology that keeps you connected to your work and other demands every minute of the day. These devices promised to allow you to do more in less time, but as far as I can see, the promise of increased leisure time is a joke.

All I ever hear in my workshops is how little time people have to do everything they're supposed to and that whatever free time they have now is constantly interrupted by their BlackBerry or cell phone. It's no wonder we eat to ease our stress.

3. Is Your Brain Overstressed?

Joan Borysenko, Ph.D., and other pioneers in mind/body medicine have spent many years conducting research showing how our minds help create many of our illnesses. This work grew into a field known as "psychoneuroimmunology."

Neuroscientists can now actually see the effects of stress on the brain: through MRIs, they're able to examine how excess stress can compromise areas like the hippocampus (the seat of memory and learning) and also the amygdala, which helps control emotions. (The amygdala reacts strongly to emotionally charged events, either very positive or very negative. Individuals who are chronically stressed have an overactive amygdala.)

Neuroscientist Bruce McEwen has written about the effects of stress on the brain and body in his book *The End of Stress as We Know It.* He states:

> With chronic stress, neurons in the amygdala grow, they become larger, and there's evidence that in depressive illness, the amygdala may even become larger, and it certainly becomes more active. After exposure to chronic stress, your hippocampus may shrink and your amygdala might grow. As a result you can have all kinds of anxieties and fears, and yet you won't have a hippocampus that can connect you to where you were and what you were doing, so you may have generalized anxiety as a result.

Too much stress can also turn off the prefrontal cortex, which results in a drop in cognitive abilities. The result is that you may lose a significant ability to control your emotions. Emotional intelligence is necessary to ensure that you react rationally to life's ups and downs, including making sensible, healthy decisions about what and how much you eat.

This may sound overly scientific, but I'm of the opinion that understanding the specific details of how our brain and body function allows us to live with less stress and make more intelligent choices. I'm fascinated by the fact that we can retrain our brain to serve us rather than make ourselves the servant to a brain that has been inadequately programmed.

A recent study published by Richard Davidson, a neuroscientist at the University of Wisconsin–Madison, pinpointed this very concept. Studying a group of Buddhist monks who were longtime practitioners of meditation, Davidson found that their mental practice had an effect on their brains similar to the way that repeated practice in a sport will improve performance. He said, "It demonstrates that the brain is capable of being trained and physically modified in ways few people can imagine." This type of research is so exciting because it disproves the theory that we're stuck with a certain way of thinking.

The last decade has uncovered amazing insights into the human mind. We now know that the brain has the ability for ongoing development and neuroplasticity. Davidson further states that "the trained mind, or brain, is physically different from the untrained one." Some of the techniques in this book can be used to train your brain in these ways so that you can increase your ability to live a happy, healthy, and fit lifestyle.

4. Are You Sleep Deprived?

We live in a society that has somehow come to feel that sleep is a waste of time. It's not uncommon to hear people brag about how little sleep they need in order to function. Is this really something to be proud of, though? I often wonder why we're so invested in convincing ourselves that surfing the Internet, returning text messages, or watching our big-screen TVs is more important than resting. Sleep deprivation creates a stress response that induces the release of cortisol, which has been found to increase abdominal fat. It also compromises memory. (So what's the point of doing so much so late in the day when you won't remember what you did, anyway?)

Remember, too much cortisol is *not* a good thing. In ancient times, it was the body's trigger to store fat in response to the famine that might follow an attack by a behemoth or saber-toothed tiger. Scientists have also found that a lack of adequate sleep (even after as little as two nights) increases the levels of the hunger hormone *ghrelin* by 28 percent, which seems to fuel our desire for carbohydrate-rich foods such as cake, candy, ice cream, pasta, and bread. In addition, insufficient sleep reduces our production of *leptin*—a protein hormone that suppresses appetite. So that's a double whammy!

Surveys estimate that 63 percent of American adults don't get the recommended eight hours of sleep each night. Many of us just don't have a good sense of how much sleep we really need, but Eve Van Cauter, a University of Chicago sleep researcher, recommends the following formula: "In general most adults need seven to nine hours a night. There are some who can do with less, and others who need more. The next time you're on vacation, sleep as much as you can the first couple of days. That way you can pay off your sleep debt. Then, when your sleep has stabilized, record how much you sleep, plus or minus 15 minutes. This is your sleep need or capacity."

I wish people would heed this advice—not only for their own well-being, but for mine and everyone else's. I'm sick and tired of being around folks who always complain about how tired they are. Isn't that infuriating? Yet it seems as if that's a rote response these days. When casually asked how they're doing, people used to respond with: "Oh, I'm fine." But now it's always: "Oh, I'm *so* tired!" I feel like yelling, "Then go get some sleep for God's sake!"

5. What's Your Role in It?

I've often said: *I have seen the enemy, and it is me.* If only we could embrace this ideology—but it's not easy to accept our own insanity. It's much easier to always be on the look-out for the thing or person or event that drove us to overeat, or to not exercise or manage stress. Most of us don't realize that one of the most insidious characteristics of self-defeating behavior is that it guarantees the consequences that we're trying to avoid.

I used to believe that many of my feelings were the direct result of other people's behaviors; in other words, that *they* (whoever "they" are) made me upset, so I was stuck in the situation as long as those people (or a specific person) were in my life, or I had to try to change them. I saw no other way to perceive the situation. This type of thinking is, of course, absurd. It forces us to constantly obsess about how we're going to change others—a thing that we have absolutely no power to do. What a waste of time! But many of us are experts in making ourselves crazy by talking to ourselves in irrational ways.

I'd often get upset because my children didn't help me with the chores. My mantra was: "No one ever helps me!" Well, yeah. My kids already knew that; that's why they were sitting around having fun, and I was getting more and more exhausted. Now in this case, I actually had a little power because they were my kids—I could coerce them to pick up the slack. But suppose we were talking about co-workers? How many of us obsess over how little other people do to help us on a daily basis?

Or what about the little things your spouse does that drive you crazy? I've heard people in my workshops talk about their extreme levels of stress and anxiety over everything from dirty clothes left on the floor, change being jangled around in a pocket, and lights left on in a vacant room . . . to bills being paid late.

How many extra pounds of potato chips have been consumed due to these sorts of stressors? So, we know that we all make choices that can lead to us becoming stressed out and slothful. What do we need to do to change this?

Assess Where You Are

You can't move forward until you look at what keeps you stuck. I've created a list of questions, and I'd like you to answer them as fully and truthfully as you can. Keep in mind that many of us practice "untidy thinking," meaning that we have the ability to fool ourselves a lot of the time in order to support our unhealthy habits. You may want to do this assessment with a trusted friend or significant other so that you can see it from a different vantage point.

The point of this self-assessment isn't to get a certain "score"; it's simply a way for you to think hard about the things in your life that might be holding you back. Seeing clearly is the first task you must undertake before you can start making changes.

Self-Assessment

As you read the following questions, take your time and think about your responses thoroughly. Most important, be honest. Write down your answers in your journal or in a notebook.

1. How long have you been overweight? Underexercised? Stressed out? (Answer all that apply.)

2. How much time do you spend talking or thinking about these issues without really doing something about them?

3. Are members of your family or your friends in the same predicament? If so, how many? And how often do you discuss it with them?

4. Have you ever tried to write down the reasons why you're not thinner, calmer, or more fit?

5. Does your closet contain a wide variety of sizes of clothes that you either fit into at one time, fit into now, or think you'll fit into later?

6. Can you recognize what triggers your over-eating, underexercising, or increased anxiety?

7. Have you ever spoken to a therapist, nutritionist, or personal trainer to help get you on track? If not, why? (If the reasons are financial, have you ever tried to take advantage of Internet sites that can offer advice in the same areas without charge?)

8. Are there people in your life who sabotage your success in these areas either through innuendo or overt comments? (Sometimes people don't really want you to change.)

9. When you discuss your health, do you continually denigrate or fault yourself for not being successful? Do you focus on your failures rather than celebrating minor successes?

10. Do you have a list of excuses for why nothing ever works for you?

11. Do you feel that your life isn't what you expected it to be? Are you disappointed in how it has turned out?

12. Are you tired a lot?

13. Does your mind jump around, as if a bunch of monkeys are in there searching for a banana?

14. Are your kitchen cabinets filled with junk foods?

15. Do fruits and vegetables sound like a foreign language?

16. If you were to name one or two people in your life who really support your well-being, who would they be?

17. Do you have a significant other and/or children who would benefit if you were in a healthier place?

18. Are you the caretaker of your (or your spouse's) mother, father, or both?

19. Do you like your job? If not, what about it stresses you out?

20. How long is your commute to work? In addition to that, do you have to drive parents or kids to doctors' appointments or other activities? How much time does that take per week?

21. Do you sleep well? If not, how often do you lie awake or get up to go to the bathroom?

22. How's your sex life? (Remember, you don't have to have a partner to have a good sex life. A partner is a nice thing—but where there's a will, there's a way!)

23. Is your home conducive to your being able to find a quiet space to renew yourself periodically, or is there constant noise and chaos?

24. How many minutes (or hours) are you talking on your cell phone, checking e-mail, or surfing the Internet?

25. How much television do you watch? (Being overweight and the number of hours that you're glued to the set have a direct correlation.)

26. Have you ever kept a food diary? If not, why?

27. Do you have any idea how many calories you consume in a day?

28. When is the last time you weighed yourself?

29. Do you participate in any type of physical activity? (Getting out of bed isn't an aerobic activity, but it's a beginning.)

30. What are your health goals, and in what time frame would you like to achieve them? (Be realistic. Trying to lose 50 pounds in a month isn't going to work—unless you have your head cut off.)

Develop Tools to Reduce Stress

We must learn to become better at recognizing our thought traps. Most of us have no clue how crazy we make ourselves, especially when it comes to weight issues, exercise, and stress. Over the years, I've heard excuses that range from the sublime to the ridiculous. Nothing can change if we don't first change the way we think about things.

If you believe that you'll never be happy or successful, then no matter what you do, you won't ever feel happy or successful. This is because you focus all your energy on being right. If you believe that certain people or events create your difficulties, then you'll spend your time trying to change them, which is a pointless exercise. The thing that needs to change is the way you see your obstacles. You need to focus on how you perceive the world. Francis of Assisi said it best: "Who we are looking for is who is looking."

Here are some common thought traps:

— *Jumping to conclusions.* You make assumptions even though you don't have any relevant information. For example, you walk into a clothing store and the clerk is looking at you intently. You assume she's noticed that your stomach is sticking out and that she's thinking, *God, I hope she's not looking for pants. We have nothing that will fit her!* In the meantime, however, she walks up to you and says, "I really like the belt you're wearing. Did you get it here?" There goes that assumption.

When you feel this coming on, see if you can think of alternative possibilities to counter the negative ones you've imagined. Even silly ones. The point is just to break the pattern. For instance, in the scene I just described, you could imagine that the clerk was thinking: *God, doesn't she look just like Catherine Zeta-Jones,* or *It's time for my break—she can get her pants elsewhere,* or *Yahoo! Three more hours of hell!* Make yourself laugh; it will defuse the bad thoughts.

— *Magnifying and minimizing.* You dwell on the bad stuff and minimize the good stuff. For example, someone at work tells you that you look good, and you answer, "Not really—I have a long way to go." Or you have five more pounds to lose to reach your goal, but you discuss it as if you were the Goodyear Blimp and have no hope of ever losing it.

Can you possibly just say "Thank you"? Try it—it feels great!

— *Personalizing.* Anything and everything can happen to you, and it's all your fault. For example, there has been an outbreak of salmonella in your child's school, and you're sure that it's because you didn't wash your hands long enough before preparing kids' lunches for the spring picnic. All this does is perpetuate guilt and depression.

When you start to feel this way, try the technique of taking a negative thought to the extreme, such as: *Yes, the children will all end up hospitalized, and the police will go from house to house checking hands. They'll find me and cart me off, as my neighbors throw stones at me and then dance about while singing "Ding-dong, the witch is dead!"*

The sillier your scenario is, the more you'll help yourself see how your negative thoughts might also be a bit silly.

— *Externalizing.* This is the flip side of personalizing. Now it's someone else's fault. For example, you blame others for your poor eating habits: "How can I ever lose weight when Mom insists on bringing a cheesecake to dinner every week? She knows I can't resist it!" This does nothing but make you a constant victim. I'd have to say this is one of the most prevalent thought traps.

It's sometimes hard to do, but you *do* have to take into account your role in the situation. You might have to face the truth: that you mother may bring the cheesecake, but she doesn't tie you down and shove it down your throat.

— *Mind reading.* I love this one, and it's amazing how often this type of thinking manifests. This is when you seem to think that you have access to other people's thoughts or actions. For example, you *know* that while your brother-in-law is watching television, he's looking at you out of the corner of his eye and thinking, *Her ass is the size of a house.*

If you consider yourself psychic, then get an 800 number and start a business. Otherwise, here's my favorite bit of advice: *Just stop it!*

— *The rescue mentality.* You hope that someone (or something) will somehow magically change your life so that you can take better care of yourself. This is one of the greatest myths that women fall prey to. For example, you may find yourself thinking, *When I get a new job, I'll have time to exercise* or *I'll lose weight when there's a man who's interested in me.*

Guess what? No one's coming! This hasn't been an easy lesson for me, either. It has taken me years to realize that *I* am my own knight in shining armor.

Relax Your Body and Mind

Stress creates a vicious cycle. As our thoughts become more irrational, our bodies become more tense, leading to increased anxiety. There has been a great deal of information on how quieting the mind can help relieve stress, but we often don't realize how tense our bodies have become and how that negatively affects our state of mind.

I encourage you to relax your mind and body at the same time with a technique called "progressive relaxation." Be aware, though, that people who always like to be in control sometimes find that these types of exercises can actually *increase* their stress level. Yet do allow yourself to try it a few times before you give up.

Progressive Relaxation

Find a comfortable position, either lying on the floor or sitting in a chair. Keep your back straight and your feet flat on the floor (if you're sitting up), with your arms resting comfortably in your lap or at your sides. Try not to obsess over the perfect pose—just get comfortable.

Close your eyes (or keep them open if you have a hard time keeping them shut), and slowly breathe in and out. As you tense your muscles, you'll inhale deeply. Hold the tension, take a few breaths, and then release all the tension as you exhale.

Start with your feet: Intentionally curl your toes to create tension, and hold this for a count of 15. Then slowly let go and wiggle them around. Create tension in your lower legs by squeezing the muscles, hold for a count of 15, and then let go. Repeat this for your thighs, buttocks, hands, forearms, shoulders, back, and neck. Take a one-minute break after each muscle group. Each time you release tension, think of doing it like a cat would . . . slowly and deeply. Continue to gently breathe throughout the exercise. Enjoy each breath as you would anything else that you deem pleasurable in your life.

You might enjoy using music as a companion to this exercise. I highly recommend works by Dean Evenson, which I find really lovely and use to help me unwind. One of my favorites is called the *Tao of Healing*. (You can order his music from Soundings of the Planet: 1-800-93-PEACE or **www.sound ings.com**.)

If you become adept at progressive relaxation, you can do mini-versions of it at any time or just breathe deeply whenever you're becoming aggravated. The object is to interrupt the stress cycle so that you have time to make healthy choices rather than immediately overreacting and grabbing a handful of cookies.

Your body holds memories of past traumas, pain, anger, and sadness. As you train your mind and body to recognize and appreciate the feeling of relaxing tension, you'll notice that you experience less anxiety. Your brain will become less reactive. Give yourself permission to enjoy the process. There will always be some pressing thing to be done for your business or a family member who needs your attention, but sometimes you have to allow yourself to come first.

"If you ask me what the single most important key to longevity is, I would have to say it is avoiding worry, stress, and tension. And if you didn't ask me, I'd still have to say it."

— George Burns

CHAPTER SEVEN

The Strength Pantry

"If you're still alive, it's not too late."

When Dr. Martin Seligman began publishing his books on positive psychology, I was totally enamored with the principles he was writing about. They completely fit in with what I've believed and been teaching over the years. I loved the fact that someone was finally saying "Enough already!" to our scientific community's obsession with dysfunctional behavior. How about we focus on what makes people function well?! Why aren't we studying the most effective individuals in our society so that we can reach those high standards? Instead, scientists research diseases and disorders and then try to help people avoid them. That shows us how to avoid severe illnesses, but what about reaching our highest potential?

Seligman's research in optimism led him to establish the field of positive psychology, which has taken on tremendous momentum in contemporary thinking on human potential and is clearly making a difference in helping people create more fulfilling lives. He doesn't say that you should gloss over your problems or pretend that you don't have issues that are keeping you stuck. However, there's a limit to how much positive change you can effect by constantly focusing on how your parents were less than perfect or by talking about how little willpower you have. That doesn't help you attain the life you desire.

I've always loved showing people what they *could* accomplish in a given situation rather than what they *couldn't*. However, I was never a Pollyanna about it because my personal style has always been a little uneven when it comes to how I live my own life. I can whine and make myself crazy over a lot of little things—and sometimes I sound like the people I tease at my seminars who "catastrophize" and "awfulize." But at the same time, I'm really masterful at focusing on my goals and accomplishments.

Although I teach how to manage stress by using humor as a coping mechanism—in addition to the tenets of positive psychology—I know that it's extremely difficult to change who we are at the core of our being. Think about how many years some of us have been practicing how to make ourselves miserable and the vast number of ways in which people live in dysfunction. So many of today's self-help books tell us to think positively, say certain phrases, do certain rituals, and on and on. Sure, some of it works and I've certainly espoused a great deal of it, but these simple solutions don't work for everyone, nor do they work in every situation.

There are physical and mental illnesses such as clinical depression, bipolar disorder, and schizophrenia that may need to be managed with medication. There are also behaviors that stimulate the pleasure centers of the brain to excess; and for some people, that leads to engaging in uncontrollable extremes, including alcoholism and compulsive gambling, shopping, or overeating. That's why addiction is so hard to treat. Once the button gets pushed in an individual who has the biological predisposition to get hooked, it starts a tsunami of wanting.

Even if you don't have the wiring, I'd be amazed to find that you haven't been acculturated on some level to reward yourself with something that feels or tastes good. Most parents don't reward their kids with a pet tarantula for getting good grades. In my day, it was an ice-cream cone or some pizza. And a lot of us still use food as a way to stay motivated.

Whatever it is that pushes your buttons, using positive psychology makes so much sense. It's fine to acknowledge your frailties—in fact, it's important to understand where your weaknesses lie. But then move on and focus on your successes. I actually think it works best when you acknowledge your strong and weak points together.

Give it a try. See if you can spend a few days really trying to honor the things that are your strengths. It can be harder than you think, so feel free to mix it up. You just may be the type who finds it tough to write or talk about yourself in positive ways. So go ahead and wallow in it: tell people how you've given up on losing weight, how you just can't seem to stick to an exercise program, or that you're a dismal failure at meditating. But then make sure that you also say at least one positive thing about yourself, even if it's as simple as "I got out of bed today."

If you're an out-of-control whiner, learn how to manage it. Make a game of it, and keep a timer with you: Give yourself ten minutes to get it out of your system. Fill your friends in on the game, and see what happens. But the unbreakable rule is that at the end of the ten minutes, you have to have said at least one great thing about yourself. This may be difficult, and you may never be a role model for positive thinking or the guru of enlightenment, but you can certainly shift some of your thinking and perhaps even some of your behaviors. You have to begin to tap into your strengths . . . and like any good pantry, the goods will be there for your taking.

10 Strengths to Dip Into to
Lose Weight and Reduce Stress

1. Ask the Right Questions in the Best Possible Way

Over the years, many people have shared a great deal of their problems with me. A lot of them have suffered profusely as the result of poor choices. Whether it's weight gain, problems with a partner, job difficulties, or numerous other issues, one of the root causes of making poor choices is the inability to ask ourselves the proper questions. We'd much rather spend our energy coming up with excuses for why we made the poor choices to begin with.

The questions we ask internally (those that are part of our inner conversations) and the ones we ask externally (to those around us) steer our behaviors and therefore our experiences. There are times when I've driven myself insane by repeatedly going over the same question about a specific situation. What makes me believe that if I become obsessed by it I'll somehow miraculously receive the answer I'm looking for? There are many well-known terms for this type of thinking, and I'm sure you've heard them: *stinking thinking, magical thinking, automatic thinking,* or *irrational thinking.* No matter what you call it, the outcome is always the same: You don't come out a winner.

Have you ever wondered about the following:

- *What I should eat today*

- *How I gained this weight*

- *If I should go for a walk today or forget about it till tomorrow*

- *When I'll have some time for myself*

Well, I'll wonder with you, but it won't do either of us any good. It just makes you spin your wheels without providing any direction. It merely sounds as if you're in limbo. This isn't a healthy way to create a feeling of self-worth. It simply implies that any old answer will do and that you're at the mercy of your own inadequacies.

Asking the right question in the best possible way will help penetrate your denial system. And the best possible question is a positive one. This isn't some airy-fairy means of communicating; it allows you to get a response that's in alignment with what you're seeking to enhance, which is better health and well-being. The *Encyclopedia of Positive Questions* provides one definition of this type of question: "A positive question is an affirmatively stated question—a question that seeks to uncover and bring out the best in a person, a situation or an organization. It is constructed around a topic that . . . is fundamentally affirmative."

You want to have the best possible day filled with energy and enthusiasm, so why not start the day by asking yourself: *What would be the healthiest thing I could eat for breakfast that would increase my vitality and get me through the day?* I doubt that you're going to respond with: *I think I'll have two burgers topped with cheese, bacon, and a big serving of fries!* You might, but then as my mother often said, "You never know." At least you'll find out how serious you are about making the right choices.

2. Think about When You've Been Successful and Which Skills Made It Possible

Most of us have an incredible ability to remain fixed on what's *not* working for us. If I regret any one thing in my life, it's the time I've spent "self-flagellating." And I'm not alone—many of us have an internal whip that we keep beating ourselves up with.

It's easy to fall into this, especially when you've had a history of old inner messages that have continually made you feel like you're not "okay" or "normal." However, if you went to school, graduated, held down a job, raised children, or have had good relationships; or if you've done something as simple as get out of bed and dressed yourself, you've created skills that have allowed you to persevere. What are they? I know one of mine is tenacity. It has been my greatest strength . . . at times, however, it has also kept me stuck. You have to know when to hang on and when to let go.

Think about your successes and how you attained them. Don't be shy about this. In your journal or in a notebook, write down everything that comes to mind as you assess your own strengths. For example:

- *I'm a good writer.*
- *I can paint.*
- *I have good intuition.*
- *I'm well organized.*
- *I'm a good listener.*
- *I did a great job raising my kids.*
- *I'm a terrific boss.*
- *I solve problems creatively.*
- *I have a great sense of style.*

3. Have a Vision

This may sound crazy if you're not familiar with visualization techniques, but bear with me. How do you see yourself? What "photograph" of yourself do you carry around in your head?

Many of us have created distorted images of ourselves. Women in particular have been taught to view themselves with a very critical eye. Over the years, I've coached beautiful, fit women whose primary focus (and obsession) had become getting rid of a sprinkling of cellulite on their thighs. It's as if the rest of them had disappeared.

If you discuss how you look or feel in negative terms, chances are that you also have strong feelings that resonate with those thoughts. You need to change your mental image in order to change your negative beliefs. I know it's easier said than done. If you think this is *too* difficult, however, find a photo of yourself when you really felt great about how you looked and felt, and use that to reform your self-image. If that's not possible, cut out some pictures that could realistically portray how you want to look. However, if you're 5'2" and curvy, then choosing an image of a six-foot-tall model who resembles a broomstick is *not* going to serve you. Seek out realistic pictures, not ones that are unattainable. It will only make you feel more inadequate.

This technique is often used by athletes to help them get to the top of their game. A friend of mine from Boston who was on the Olympic rowing team several years ago told me that visualization was a big part of her training. Her coach would get the team out on the Charles River every morning at 5:30 and have them visualize themselves rowing to victory. I've used this technique when I'm really on a roll with getting myself into a healthier place—and *it works.* (Check out Health Journeys, a company created by Belleruth Naparstek, which has all kinds of visualization CDs that I know can help you.)

4. Create a Support Group

I know that "group consciousness" can make a huge difference in whether a person fails or succeeds at something. How many hours do you think you've spent trying to convince other people that you aren't good at something by sharing all your weaknesses? Women are so adept at this, spending hours talking about failed weight loss, broken relationships, unruly children . . . blah, blah, blah.

It's okay to vent, and to laugh at some of the crazy stuff that creeps into your life—but outside of that, put a lid on it! Get together with your friends periodically to see how you can surmount obstacles, not make more of them. It will be hard because it goes against most people's instincts, but if you have a group that understands the rules, it's easier. You have to be willing to talk about what you want to accomplish, the goals you've set for yourself, and the strengths you bring to the table. Let everyone talk freely. Listen, don't interrupt, and take notes. Sometimes someone who isn't invested in your excuses can make a real difference in your life.

5. Challenge Yourself

We live in a world where everyone expects things to come quickly and easily. God forbid we should have to wait a few extra minutes for a cup of coffee or have to put up with traffic. Fast-food restaurants have become a metaphor for life: *Get it fast and easy!* It just may well be that as we've gone down this road, we've lost something along the way. Consider the following startling facts:

- Rates of depression have risen in recent decades, at the same time that people are enjoying time-saving conveniences such as microwave ovens, e-mail, prepared meals, and machines for washing clothes and mowing lawns.

- People of earlier generations, whose lives were characterized by greater efforts just to survive, paradoxically, were mentally healthier. [Our] human ancestors also evolved in conditions where hard physical work was necessary to thrive.

- By denying our brains the rewards that come from anticipating and executing complex tasks with our hands . . . we undercut our mental well-being. (*Scientific American Mind,* August/September 2008)

Evidently, we'd feel a deep sense of satisfaction when true physical and mental effort produces something tangible. Wouldn't it be interesting if the reason why so many of these diets in a box and other so-called easy weight-loss plans that we hear about day in and day out fail exactly because they're *too* easy? Maybe the real success in staying well mentally and physically is in discovering that the mind and body *like* effort. Perhaps that's what makes us thrive and survive!

6. Set Positive Goals

Making a commitment to yourself to look and feel better allows you to identify the barriers to your success and then realistically problem-solve. It takes effort to begin this process, but it can also be exciting and fulfilling.

Setting goals gives you something to strive for. In fact, everyone creates goals, both good and bad. You may not believe that there are goals associated with your bad habits, but if you smoke, for example, getting to the store before you run out of cigarettes is a goal (obviously not a good one). If you like potato chips, you're going to make sure that you always have a lot of them around. If you overeat in secret, it can take a lot of effort to plan the deception and hide the evidence.

So you no doubt understand the concept; you just have to switch gears. Try starting with short-term goals if larger ones seem scary. Take a little bit of the effort you took in planning to overeat, and plan differently. If you've been eating meat every night, substitute fish or a vegetable stir-fry for one of the nights. If you don't get much exercise, try taking just a half hour one day to walk or bike or do whatever floats your boat.

7. Take Action—Then Talk about It

There's no perfect time to begin anything—you just have to start doing it. Obsessing about all the times it didn't work isn't going to get you anywhere, and it certainly won't inspire you to get going. As Nike has often stated: "Just do it"!

You can only embody what you want to create, not what you want to eliminate. Changing your actions first is one way to bring your desired goals to fruition. You may fail again and again, but studies have shown that stopping bad habits often takes two years of contemplation and then a few more years to establish the positive behavior you're striving for. Look at how many years it took you to create an unhealthy lifestyle! It's only by taking action that you can discover and create what works in the present.

The majority of us love to talk about what we're going to do. I can't tell you how many times I've said, "I need to lose weight." If I had simply spent the time I talked about my desire to lose weight by eating less and walking more, it would be a moot issue.

Our fears get in the way, and we end up talking about what we're going to do instead of actually doing it. We need to try the trial-and-error approach. This is what children do: no little kid ever comes in the house and says, "I've been thinking about jumping up and down, and then rolling around on the lawn for a bit." They just do it! Somehow as we get older, our internal critics take over and tell us not to act because we may be wasting time or may look foolish. But is anything more of a waste than continuing to do nothing?

Don't wait! You may die first, and then you'll be the thinnest person around.

Start a Fun Food Journal

You know that keeping a food journal is a great way to monitor what you eat, as well as provide yourself with a record to look back on if you need to see where you've been going wrong. But wouldn't it be fun to also keep a journal of the things that you love about your food each day? Calorie counting is one thing; how about counting the pleasure you get from your meals?

I bet if you take some time to really focus on what it is about certain foods that give you the most pleasure, it will be easier to spot when you're mindlessly shoveling down Doritos.

For example:

- With lunch, I had the most luscious ripe tomato cut into slices with a little olive oil and salt. Heavenly!

- I took a trip to the farm stand, where a local baker had just delivered fresh wheat rolls flavored with rosemary. I ate two—they were so savory they didn't even need butter.

- I met Josephine for breakfast at the diner and ordered pancakes, which were probably a little too extravagant, but they were so light and fluffy that they were worth it. Still, I ate only about half of what was on my plate.

8. Do It with Some Energy!

I always find it interesting that when people talk about getting into better shape, they usually sound depressed and anxious. It's rare to hear a person say, "I'm so excited! I've decided to make my lifestyle healthier, so I can really enjoy everything I do to the fullest." I think that most people are so used to living as if their batteries need charging that they don't realize they can feel a lot better.

I don't think a day goes by without someone telling me they're tired. It's gotten to be almost epidemic. Primary-care physicians have reported that that is the number one complaint they hear from patients. Yes, life has become more complex, and most of us work too hard and don't get enough sleep. But packing on pounds, being stressed out, and not getting enough exercise make it all so much worse.

You can't imagine how much more energy you'll have when you get going and do it with a joyful outlook.

9. Tap Into Your Altruism

At one time or another, you've probably donated money to charities or volunteered your service as a way to express your generosity and empathy for others. Yet have you thought of the possibility that taking care of your own mental and physical well-being could be one of the greatest contributions you could make to your fellow humans?

When you're in good health, you tax the health-care system less; stay independent longer; and are a positive role model for family members, friends, and co-workers. If there are any individuals in my audience who have decided to simply ignore the signals of their poor health, I ask if they've had a family gathering of late in order to assign someone as their caretaker. Not for a crisis, but for the long term. If you've gotten very out of shape and been living an unhealthy lifestyle, it's likely that one day, even just going to the store for some groceries will become a problem. Who's going to volunteer their time to help you?

It's essentially a selfish act not to consider that other lives will be compromised if you don't pay attention to your health.

10. Use Your Compassion

The majority of us seem to have compassion for others when we sense that they've gone through hard times or tragedies. This is one of our greatest assets as human beings. However, it's often more difficult to feel it for ourselves. It takes courage and resiliency to make positive changes in our lives.

The amount of success you have will depend on your ability to forgive yourself with compassion if you hit the wall or don't meet your goals. Try not to berate yourself or indulge in guilty self-talk. That behavior won't serve you. You'll only end up feeling like a failure . . . and then what?

*"Once we believe in ourselves, we can risk
curiosity, wonder, spontaneous delight, or
any experience that reveals the human spirit."*

— E. E. Cummings

CHAPTER EIGHT

The Now of Chow

*"Eat, drink, and be merry—but don't
do anything else at the same time."*

One of the most important aspects of eating is to "be with the food." A lot has been written about being in the present moment and how important that is when it comes to living a fulfilling life. Yet many of us see food as something that gets in the way of our never-ending to-do lists. Why else would we have so many fast-food restaurants; so many ways to get takeout; and so many people mindlessly eating while they drive, sit at their desks, or talk on their cell phones?

There's a ritual attached to eating that was once a huge part of dining. As a child, I always delighted in going food shopping with my grandmother. This ritual combined all the elements of a great novel: there was drama, comedy, and a cast of unforgettable characters. And there was no such thing as one-stop shopping, nor did we jump into the car to quickly get it done. There was either a little cart we dragged behind us as we walked, or we'd bring along net bags that we hoped would be big enough to handle whatever we bought.

Grandma Francesca and I would walk several blocks to the shops and methodically go in and out of each one, buying ingredients for the next couple of days' meals. There was the butcher, the cheese shop, the vegetable and fruit market, and my favorite: the stand where you could get Italian ice. I loved the little white cup chock-full of flavored ice that you kept sucking on until it was down to the bottom. We never checked to see how much time our shopping trip was taking because there were important decisions to make. Francesca had to have the most tender veal for her veal cutlets, the freshest arugula and tomatoes for her salad, and grating cheese that had a bite to it. She would have been horrified by the idea of taking home pre-grated cheese in a container. You picked out a good, fragrant solid cheese, took home a piece, and grated it yourself.

The Joy of Food

There are some terrific movies that depict the ecstasy of eating in a highly sexual way. One of my favorites is the classic *Tom Jones.* Who could forget the infamous dining scene when Joyce Redman's and Albert Finney's characters were sitting across from each other eating pears, biting into each one slowly and methodically while the juice spurted from the fruit and dribbled down the front of their clothing? It left such an impression on me that years later, when I was in the beginning stages of a love affair and spending the night in a hotel, I tried to replicate the experience. I wore a sexy black negligee and ordered every dessert on the room-service menu. My then-lover and I sat in bed totally naked devouring chocolate mousse, crème caramel, chocolate-covered strawberries, ice cream, and baked Alaska while we delighted in carnal pleasures.

Rent one of these films, and you'll savor the experience!

- *Babette's Feast*
- *Chocolat*
- *Eat Drink Man Woman*
- *Mostly Martha*
- *Like Water for Chocolate*
- *Big Night*
- *Tampopo*

As Grandma and I walked the neighborhood, we'd often see a lot of familiar faces in the stores doing similar errands. Unlike these days, our neighbors were folks we usually knew quite well, and we'd stop and chat with them. If we were in the butcher shop, someone would give my grandmother a much-loved recipe for a special sauce ragu. If we were at the vegetable stand, it was a recipe for salad dressing. Neighborhood women always shared recipes and cooking tips.

What I remember the most about food shopping was how much fun it was. I'm sure there are still neighborhoods where this goes on, but for the most part, Americans have lost the art of being connected to their food in the same way our grandparents or parents were. Now we usually go to one supermarket and take whatever they have, whether or not it's up to our standards. It's just too inconvenient to look elsewhere. We often mindlessly fill up our carts, with the primary goal being to get out of there as soon as possible.

One of the ways we could get in touch with what we eat and become more mindful about food is to try to re-create our grandparents' customs. We need to pay attention to all the luscious scents, textures, and tastes of what we put in our mouths.

In an era of down-and-dirty dining, many of us have forgotten how food not only fuels us, but also how it feeds our senses. It can conjure up powerful memories, both good and bad, and bring us in touch with our ethnicity. Sharing a meal has the power to help us do business, connect family and friends, and share a romantic evening as a prelude to more. Let's stop talking about food as if we were emergency-room physicians. Let's focus on the texture and taste of summer tomatoes, not just on their lycopene levels and antioxidant properties.

I'm not saying that we shouldn't be conscious of the nutritional values of what we eat, of course. But we do need to think about food in a less clinical way. Can't we find a balance? I hope so. Let's start by trying to regain the connection to our sensual past. Children are acutely aware of tasting, touching, smelling, seeing, and hearing—how often are adults so in touch with their senses? When we are, we actually tend to slow down and savor what's around us, including the food we eat.

Tune In to Your Senses

Jon Kabat-Zinn is one of the leading authorities in mindfulness meditation and a leading expert in mind-body studies. I'll never forget the first time I heard him speak: one of the exercises he conducted with the audience was to get everyone to eat a raisin for a half hour. This isn't an easy thing to do! Most people had an incredibly hard time with it because the majority of us swallow as fast as we can so that we can take the next bite.

Now I'm not suggesting that you should make raisins your new best friend, but perhaps you can begin to experience more mindfulness in the way you approach food.

Try the following exercise. Close your eyes, and visualize and truly experience:

- The smell of freshly baked bread

- The last passionate kiss you experienced

- The taste of your favorite dessert

- The feel of sand between your toes

- The scent of autumn leaves

- Holding hands with a loved one

- Looking into your pet's eyes

- One of your favorite family gatherings—
  and the foods you ate together

Right now, take a moment to remember the physical pleasures inherent in those items, bringing the sensations back as if you were experiencing them again. Take some time to reconnect with what it feels like to touch something or someone—not in a perfunctory way, but with meaning and intention. After all, touch is thought to be ten times more potent than verbal or emotional contact.

Be sure to try the following:

- When you get dressed, feel each piece of clothing as you put it on. Is it rough, smooth, or silky?

- Go up to a tree and touch the bark. Run your hands up and down the trunk, feeling the bumpiness.

- When you're in the vegetable section of your grocery store, touch the skins of the fruits and vegetables. Focus on the different textures: grainy, smooth, silky, cottony, and so on.

- Touch a baby's skin. It's unbelievable, and there's nothing like it—silky and smooth like glass.

- Hold the hand of an elder family member. Feel the crevices and wrinkles that speak to this person's years on Earth.

We humans have an amazing ability to sniff out countless odors. That skill can help save our lives, enhance our sexuality, whet our appetites, and offer a host of other possibilities. "According to Alan Hirsch, M.D., neurological director of the Smell and Taste Treatment and Research Foundation in Chicago, when you breathe in a scent like tomato sauce, sensory signals travel from the nose through the amygdala to the hippocampus, areas of the brain linked to emotion and memory, before being identified and categorized" (*First* magazine, August 11, 2008).

This is why certain aromas can elicit so many emotional responses. Every sniff you take alerts you to the world around you. The scent of cinnamon seems to provoke men's sex drives . . . but then what doesn't?! How good is your sense of smell? Improving it (as well as your sense of taste) may help you become more discerning about what, where, and how much you eat.

Try the following exercise to help you enhance your smell potential:

- Explore your kitchen cabinets and savor the spices, extracts, and flavorings.

- Go to a perfume counter, and try to discern which scents belong to a specific fragrance.

- Sit with your morning cup of coffee in your hands, and take in the aroma before you taste it. Do you notice a difference?

- Walk into a friend's house and try to detect which odors identify her house and make it different from yours. How about your parents' or your in-laws' homes? What does your office smell like?

- Have someone blindfold you and see how many scents you can identify in your home and what they belong to.

- Do you have a clue as to what your own body smells like? It might be a good idea to find out.

A lot of distress in your life may come from excess noise. Do you think that certain sounds might make you prone to eat more, may make you more stressed, or perhaps make you feel safe and comfortable (and therefore more satisfied)?

We're assaulted so often with abnormally high decibel levels that audiologists are reporting signs of deafness in people in their 40s. Is that a surprise, though? I've been in stores and restaurants where the music is so jarring that I couldn't wait to leave. Why do I have to shout to have a conversation? I know that some restaurant owners think that loud, raucous music will make their establishments seem more hip, but who thinks this is an environment that's conducive to eating? The *1812 Overture* wouldn't be reasonable background music for a nice family meal, and neither is a dose of heavy metal. How can that be beneficial for my stress level and digestion? Obviously, it isn't—but "the beat goes on" in taking our attention away from what we're eating.

Try to discover what kind of sounds (or lack of) allow you to eat in a leisurely, enjoyable fashion.

Experience a Taste Sensation

And then there's taste . . . we're so blessed to have this sense, and we're surrounded by a bounty of flavors. The art of tasting is married to savoring—it's not merely good enough to pop something in our mouths and then wolf it down. Remember that tasting sensually allows us to slow down.

Try the following either in your imagination or for real:

- Eat a piece of warm, crusty Italian or French bread dipped in olive oil. You can choose butter or jam, if you wish—don't limit yourself. Really think about the textures and flavors.

- Sip some wine, lemonade, or iced tea. Roll it around in your mouth.

- Bite into a fabulous piece of chocolate. Chew slowly, savoring the texture and flavor.

- Recall a favorite dish from the past. Are you thinking about your mother's mashed potatoes? Grandma's apple pie? A Thanksgiving turkey? My favorite is my mom's lasagna.

There are so many ways to access the wonderful world of taste. Try visiting a deli. Could anything be more exciting? I particularly love a good Jewish deli and view the food behind the counter as if I'm at the theater. I want to sample everything, and it's so hard to choose. The half-sour pickles with an incredible mile-high pastrami sandwich on rye bread is to die for!

Go to a bakery, too. My father owned one in Brooklyn, and whenever I went there, I wanted to taste all of his delicacies. Eating a warm, fresh-baked hunk of bread, especially the end piece, is akin to having an orgasm.

I'm sure some of you are starting to think, *This woman needs therapy!* No, I just love food. Unfortunately, saying that in public these days could get someone a one-way ticket to a rehab facility.

Size Matters!

Brian Wansink, a professor at Cornell and author of the book *Mindless Eating*, has conducted fascinating studies to determine if there's a correlation between how much we eat and the size of the containers our food is served in. For example, in one study, Dr. Wansink gave moviegoers free popcorn. Some were given large containers, and others received the supersized jumbo buckets. The popcorn varied, too: some of it was fresh and delicious, some was so-so, and the rest was very stale—14 days old.

In all cases, people who had the biggest containers ate significantly more popcorn—even those who had received the horribly stale stuff. So does that mean we think that huge quantities are more appealing (even if they don't taste that great)? Or perhaps it's as Dr. Wansink believes: we tend to eat in amounts that seem culturally appropriate. As we're given bigger servings, we eat more—under the mistaken belief that the portion amount is reasonable. That should give us even more reason to be ever mindful of what we put in our mouths.

I recently had the wonderful experience of going to my local farmers' market in downtown Plymouth, Massachusetts. I was so excited to buy fresh tomatoes, corn, and the various other fruits and vegetables available. It reminded me of shopping with my grandma Francesca. Some people get excited by their iPhones, but I find great joy in slicing up a big juicy tomato and eating it with just the right amount of salt.

I must admit that I've gotten away from this type of experience over the years because of a demanding career and many other family responsibilities. However, I have the good fortune to have a dear friend who reminded me what I was missing out on. My friend Sue Sherman (who rivals Martha Stewart when it comes to cooking, decorating, and doing anything that can be made from scratch) drives all over the place looking for the freshest foods and has asked me many times to accompany her. I finally went with her after having a meal at her house one night that was so laden with the most simply beautiful and delicious array of vegetables that it almost brought me to ecstasy.

I'm sure you're thinking, *Poor thing! I guess this is what single life has done to her.* But my Italian upbringing gave me an appreciation for fine food that's close to spiritual salvation.

Perhaps this sounds crazy, but I've often been disappointed after bringing home fruits and vegetables from the grocery store. They look like the real thing, but when you bite into them, the taste and consistency is waxy and lifeless—as if they've escaped from Madame Tussauds. And what's even scarier about this stuff is that they often take a long time to rot . . . that just doesn't seem normal.

A lot of us have forgotten how great it is to buy vegetables that have just come out of the earth and still have the residue covering them. We've gotten so used to everything looking pristine and uniform that it's hard to think that a bumpy, multicolored tomato could be okay to eat. We walk up and down the aisles in supermarkets; and everything appears flawlessly fresh, lined up, and color coordinated. We've forgotten that nature just doesn't function that way.

Yes, I know it's convenient to shop in a store that has everything you need. Who wants to go from pillar to post searching for vegetables that were just picked? Well . . . I guess *I* do! I'm hooked. I even asked my friend Sue what we were going to do in the wintertime. She replied that we just won't eat tomatoes or corn, but we can make hearty soups, homemade breads and relishes; and maybe a quilt or two. I'm kidding about the quilts, but I'm up for the rest, and I hope you take some time to visit your local farmers' market. You'll love it!

The Slow-Food Movement

This might be a bit too alternative for many folks, but I'm fascinated by the growing "slow food" movement. The concept has been catching on for the last 20 years or so and sees itself as a way to counter the growing insanity of fast food, fast living, and the mass production of foods. It was started by Carlo Petrini, an Italian (no surprise to me!) who started the movement in his own country, but it now operates in 50 countries and has over 80,000 members.

The group advocates buying food locally; using fresh ingredients instead of prepackaged ones as often as possible; and slowing down the way food is prepared, chosen, and eaten. They also promote the idea of using food as a way to connect with community and family.

Here's the mission statement from Slow Food USA:

> Slow Food USA envisions a future food system that is based on the principles of high quality and taste, environmental sustainability, and social justice—in essence, a food system that is good, clean, and fair. We seek to catalyze a broad cultural shift away from the destructive effects of an industrial food system and fast life; toward the regenerative cultural, social, and economic benefits of a sustainable food system, regional food traditions, the pleasures of the table, and a slower and more harmonious rhythm of life.

You can find more information at **www.slowfoodusa .org**.

Dining in an unfamiliar ethnic restaurant allows us to expand our tastes—as well as our minds. And eating in silence may sound like a dreadful idea, but consider how little we engage in this process. When sound is absent, our senses leap into action and our ability to taste actually becomes more acute. I love a good conversation, but it's also true that sometimes a wonderful meal is made even better by our total concentration on it.

The way we choose food should also include the joy of the visual component. Again, I think it's sad that a lot of this has gone by the wayside as our drive to eat and run has taken precedence over our drive to savor things. I've spent a lot of time painting and visiting art museums; I'm very in touch with visual pleasures, and I'm often blown away by the colors that nature produces in its food palette. The shapes and hues are truly amazing.

There are times when I've bought a vegetable or fruit simply because I love the way it looks—even though I have no clue what to do with it! This makes sense considering that 70 percent of our sense receptors are located in our eyes. What if when we took our kids grocery shopping, we could instill in them an appreciation for what great works of art we've been blessed with? What a wonderful gift to pass on through the generations!

Next time you go shopping, hold the vegetables that you're considering next to one another as if you're choosing colors in a painting. Really study them. How beautiful does the yellow pepper look next to the orange carrots? The bright green basil with the deep scarlet tomatoes? The plump, red strawberries with dark, juicy blackberries? Studies have indicated that people's perception of how foods taste is influenced by their colors (regardless of whether or not there's any real difference in the taste). So make sure that it all looks good, too! Become a da Vinci of the supermarket!

"I am not a glutton—I am an explorer of food."

— Erma Bombeck

It's so easy for us to live unconsciously, simply going from one thing to another, unable to really delight in each moment because our focus is already on whatever we're supposed to be doing next. We need to lighten up, slow down the pace, and make mealtimes a vital part of our day. Food necessitates that we tap into and honor the wonder of all of our senses. Then and only then can we enjoy *the now of chow.*

CHAPTER NINE

Lose . . .
So That Others
May Gain

"Spread the weight around—it's not all about you."

Weight loss is a physical, mental, and spiritual process. You can chew on all the carrots you want, but it's also important to stop chewing out yourself and everyone around you. There are many tools and techniques in this book that can offer you some perspective and help you set healthy, realistic goals. Remember that the mind and body are connected. You can solve the hunger in your belly, but still manifest the behaviors of someone whose heart and soul are starving for love or meaning. I've met many people who are thin, attractive, and financially well-off, yet their eyes tell a different story. There's an emptiness that hasn't been fed.

To create health and well-being—which includes maintaining a proper weight, being physically fit, and having a peaceful countenance—we must scan our lives with the eyes of a compassionate witness. We often judge ourselves and others too harshly, and that makes it extremely difficult to implement positive changes.

"The real voyage of discovery consists not in seeking new landscapes, but in having new eyes."

— Marcel Proust

You must have new eyes to move forward and attain the changes you seek. With that in mind, I'd like you to answer the following questions:

1. Do you always seek to please everyone around you, even at your own expense?

2. Are you harboring any grudges against someone?

3. Have you learned to forgive and forget?

4. Do you find yourself spending a lot of time going over what went wrong in your life?

5. How often do you feel lonely or depressed?

6. Are you living the life you desire?

7. Do you feel respected and loved by those around you?

8. Do you feel at odds with yourself?

9. Are you passionate about something—this is, it excites and infuses you with joy—but feel like you can't pursue it until everyone around you figures out their lives?

10. How often do you feel like you're really having fun?

11. Have you discovered your life's purpose?

These questions take time and effort, although many of us will put off answering them or just say that we're too busy. It's amazing that we don't take time to tap into our inner wisdom to help us solve problems, yet we spend so much time bitching and moaning about how bad we look and feel.

I've often said that if I spent as much energy walking as I did talking about losing weight, I'd look like a recovering anorexic. If you're like me, you might want to seriously start paying attention to how many minutes, hours, days, or years you've used up whining.

Taking a close look at your answers will help you focus on the things you may want to change in your life, or they might help you see how strong you are in certain areas. This book can't possibly address all the issues that will be raised by your responses, so I've decided to focus this last chapter on the four most universal, useful, and empowering skills that will help you lose weight *and* your worries:

1. Learn How to Say No

*"A 'no' uttered from the deepest conviction
is better than a 'yes' merely uttered
to please, or worse, to avoid trouble."*

— Mohandas Gandhi

Tomes have been written about this issue, which seems to plague women more than men. We're beset with the "pleasing sickness." Too often, our friends and family members perceive us as the eternal caregivers. Once we've taken on the mantle of Florence Nightingale, we become best known for our "nursing" skills and are constantly called upon to help others. Most of us who exhibit this behavior also try to get people to recognize how good and kind we are by refusing to accept help ourselves.

But this stoic behavior reeks of martyrdom and will often begin to rankle everyone else because no one can really give and give without showing resentment. And eventually, others will turn a deaf ear to our whining about how oppressed we feel. It's a no-win situation.

I can remember a time when I *had* to take care of others because I thought it was the only way I'd be appreciated or loved, but that's never the way it works. Doormats are simply something for people to wipe their feet on.

Consider using this exercise to act out your own behavior. Stand in front of a mirror and do the following:

Put a forlorn expression on your face, and slump forward so that your body looks hunched over. Then say the following in a pitiful voice: "Whatever you say is all right with me! I don't need anything. I don't have any power of my own; I'm just here to do whatever I can for you. I hope you'll be happy with me—after all, if I can't make you happy, my life is meaningless."

Repeat this over and over for about three minutes and then see how you feel. What's your breathing like? Does your body feel weak? Of course, you may feel absurd acting this out, but that's what you've been doing, and it *is* absurd. This kind of behavior only disempowers you and can lead to overeating, underexercising, and a host of other unhealthy habits. It can also exacerbate many illnesses. You're worth more than this!

Now list about five situations in which you'd like to be more assertive. Think about how you wish to behave, not how you want to feel—after all, everyone wants to feel good all the time, but that just isn't possible. Practice your assertiveness on a trusted friend or relative, taking care to pick someone who hasn't enabled you in your need to care for the world. If you can't think of anyone, practice on a pet or the wall if need be. (Watch the movie *Shirley Valentine* for great tips in dialoguing with a wall.) Use phrases such as *I think, I feel,* or *I want to express my needs.* Don't get discouraged; this takes time. Your automatic reaction to a request will be "Yes, I will!" even if you feel resentful. It's going to be hard to change that reaction to something like: "I think you could do that yourself next time you're in town," or "I have to say that I feel a little taken advantage of."

If you're feeling really tentative the next time someone asks you to do something for them and you're not quite ready to say how you really feel, counter with a stopgap measure to help you think it through and create a strong response— something like: "Let me get back to you on that," or "I'm going to take some time to think about it." Or try my favorite: "I'm feeling confused right now. I'll get back to you later."

2. Handle Criticism in a Healthy Way

Most of us respond to criticism by becoming defensive, shutting down (pouting), or running away (and running toward something unhealthy, such as overeating). We develop a lot of our dysfunctional strategies as children by watching and then imitating our role models. My mother was extremely deft at verbal aikido, but my grandmother took the passive route. I became a combination of the two until I realized that neither served me well.

Learning to defuse criticism will not only empower you, but can ultimately bring you closer to a peaceful mind. Try the following techniques:

— When you receive criticism that feels accurate, simply acknowledge it and move on.

— If the criticism sounds unfair, don't make excuses or take out your sword so you can win the battle. Find something within the context of the criticism that you can agree with, even if it's something minor. Remember that the person talking to you wants the same validation you do.

For example, if your mother (or significant other) says, "You're always working. It would be nice if you spent more time with me," just respond by agreeing, "Yes, it's true—I do work a lot." Then wait for the next statement. If your mom continues nagging you, use a technique called "probing" to find out what she really wants. For instance, you can say, "I understand you think I work too much and you'd like to see more of me. I'm willing to try to do better. Do you have any ideas for things we can do together this week?"

The bottom line is that we all would like our needs met. If we use collaborative methods, we may actually get the brass ring. (Obviously, this is a vast subject, and there are no simple answers. See the Resources section for some good books that delve more deeply into this topic.)

3. Don't Wait to Have Fun

Why is everyone running around trying to figure out ways to have fun? We spend enormous amounts of time and effort trying to figure out how to relax, while spending equal amounts of time trying to accomplish more in less time. The dichotomy is insane!

What very few books in the self-help area ever address is fun. They don't let you in on the secret that you can have fun all day long if you realize that it isn't something you *seek,* but something you *are. Become the fun that you're seeking and you won't have to wait to have fun.* Stress is diminished in its presence, but most people don't understand the concept.

Essentially, fun is the art of playfulness and the ability to resonate with whatever you're doing in the best possible way. At some point, we became a nation of workaholics. If all you ever think about is going from one task to another without interruption, you've become a robot. Instead, try to do as much as you can with an attitude that's full of gratitude and joy. Yes, this may sound naïve, but trust me when I tell you that more things will go right than wrong.

I've tried this technique when I'm traveling, and amazing things have happened. Consider how often overworked employees in airports have to put up with disgruntled travelers. I start having fun by being playful with the gate agents. When they ask me how many bags I'm checking, I often respond, "Two, including me." I get huge guffaws, and sometimes I even get moved into first class! Our interaction has become more humane, and they're pleased that I'm interested in making our time together fun.

There are so many ways you can make your day more pleasant. In addition, if you're already enjoying yourself, you'll be less likely to try to medicate yourself with food. Here are some tips to help you experience more joy during everyday tasks:

- Get some karaoke music and sing in your car while you're stuck in traffic.

- Talk to the people standing next to you instead of using your cell phone when you're waiting in line.

- Let everyone you come in contact with know that you're interested in them by actively listening. When you act dismissive, it shows how uncomfortable you are with yourself.

- Do all your chores in as playful a way as possible. Squelch the old inner tape that says, "You can't have fun till the work is done!" *Please . . .* you'll be dead.

- Wake up and create a fun affirmation for the day, such as: *My day is filled with fun, joy, and humor.* Your attention follows your intention.

- Enjoy the ride when you're driving. You'll eventually get where you're going.

- Make your job as enjoyable as possible. You signed up—no one shipped you off to do forced labor. If you dislike your work, start making plans to do something else.

I realize that some of you reading this may be involved in some very serious situations, but keep in mind that fun is a state of mind, it's always there for you to tap into, and not every day is akin to a funeral procession.

4. Lose So That Others May Gain

Nothing resonates more with the human spirit than being altruistic. Americans are generous; in fact, we're unique among the world's people for the amount of money we give to charities. We aren't isolated; we tend to see our part in the larger world, and we want to help those who are less fortunate.

How about we take those instincts and use them to help ourselves get a handle on our growing obesity problem? As a people, we care about others—why do we have a harder time caring for ourselves? We dig deep when there's a tsunami or an earthquake and the world needs us. Meanwhile, we're sinking into a fissure of our own making. Could our desire to help others be a lifeline to a smaller waist? Every day people are starving to death, while we're eating much more than we need to.

So a question that might be helpful to consider is: "If I can't do this for myself, can I do it for others?" For example, as an incentive, how about donating a certain amount of money to a charity you believe in for each pound you lose? What a wonderful way to connect to the world and help others while also helping yourself.

It's been proven that giving to others makes you feel more connected, vibrant, and important in the world. The act of giving is one of the highest forms of self-actualized behavior, according to Abraham Maslow's "hierarchy of needs." To give is to feel a higher purpose: when you care about what happens to others, it increases your capacity for openness and may actually extend your life.

It just might be that the simple act of giving will be enough of an enhancement to your self-esteem that it will make responsible eating easier to do. But it also can be a terrific incentive to keep you on track.

Imagine if everyone in the U.S. donated a dollar to charity for every pound they lost—that alone would provide almost $300 million to causes that need help. But what is one pound? Or one dollar?

"If you can't feed a hundred people, then feed just one."

— Mother Teresa

Do you remember when I said that Americans are collectively overweight by five billion pounds? Well, a dollar for each of those pounds would put a lot of food on the tables of people who have nothing. Or it could solve our energy crisis. Or it would help create world-class schools throughout the country.

Think about the sorts of things that would be meaningful to you if you were to start "lightening up" to help others. Choosing a charity that holds special significance to you may well keep you invested longer and keep the project closer to your heart. It's truly a way to give a part of yourself . . . and not a part you mind giving away: your excess fat!

Do you have a relative or friend with a particular disease that you'd like to support with donations? There are numerous vital organizations that provide information and fund research for virtually every disease and illness known to humankind. The following are just some of the terrific organizations that are out there:

- American Cancer Society

- The Leukemia & Lymphoma Society

- American Heart Association

- March of Dimes (for preventing birth defects and infant mortality)

- Muscular Dystrophy Association

- American Kidney Fund

Are there social issues that are of particular importance to you—causes that you believe in strongly enough to support in this special way? Would you consider giving a part of yourself to any of the following:

- NAACP
- Gay Men's Health Crisis
- Wildlife Conservation Society
- Children's Defense Fund
- The Salvation Army
- Greenpeace
- Sierra Club
- Habitat for Humanity
- Doctors Without Borders
- Big Brothers Big Sisters

For me, I think that one of the best ways for us to take advantage of the specific nature of this kind of giving is to think of using our own ability to normalize our eating as a way to help put food in the mouths of people who don't have enough to eat. What kind of world is this when we have such bounty that our bodies are straining against it—and elsewhere people are starving? And it's not just in some far-off places; there are a lot of hungry people right here in the U.S. who desperately need help.

So as we improve our lives by eating less, others will be provided with food that will help save their lives. Isn't that an empowering idea? Talk about a win-win situation! Here are some charities that help feed people in need:

- CARE
- The Hunger Project
- Action Against Hunger
- Citymeals-on-Wheels
- Bread for the World
- Feeding America

I'm so inspired by the work of Jeffrey Sachs, an economist and director of the Earth Institute at Columbia University, who is a relentless fighter against world hunger. He wrote a book called *The End of Poverty* and began what has come to be known as the Millennium Villages project. There are now dozens of these villages throughout Africa (and elsewhere), proving that with some investment in agriculture, clean water, and education, they can sustain themselves and create enough food to feed their population. These Millennium Villages are even beginning to feed and educate neighboring villages.

Dr. Sachs says that with an investment of less than 1 percent of the GNP of the world's wealthy countries, we could end world hunger. We just need to do it smartly. We can't feed everyone; we need to help them learn how to feed themselves.

Feeding Those Who Are Close to Home

If you don't think that giving cash is the right kind of incentive for you, how about offering your time and energy to help people who need it? Being an active participant in your community is also a great way to open yourself up to the world and find ways to fill your own inner needs. Sometimes that's enough to prevent you from filling up on Colonel Sanders.

How about using your love of food to prepare and serve meals for the elderly or homeless? Every community has a church or soup kitchen that survives on volunteer help. It can be a lot of fun and a great way to meet new people, while also supporting a worthy community enterprise that truly helps those in need. And it may help remind you that for some, food is a necessity, not a form of entertainment.

If a soup kitchen isn't for you, how about teaching a cooking class for local children? Take what you know about food (and your love for it) and volunteer to show a group of kids how to prepare healthy meals that they'll enjoy. And maybe afterward, the whole group can deliver the meals you prepared together to a nursing home and complete the circle.

Or how about making a girls' night out of it? Get a group of friends together, and instead of going to a restaurant and eating and drinking too much, sit around in someone's kitchen and do something that gives back to the community. How about cooking a nice big meal that could feed some local senior citizens who are shut-ins? Or have a blast baking cakes and cookies together, and then sell them at a bake sale to raise money for a charity you decide on in advance?

Wouldn't it be fun to hang out with good friends and think of ways in which you can make a difference in the world? Group consciousness, when directed toward something worthwhile, can be extraordinary. You'll also be an incredible role model for your children and grandchildren.

I recently read an inspiring story about Olga Murray, an 82-year-old retired lawyer from California, who now spends half her time in Nepal, where she works toward freeing enslaved girls. In that society, it's a common practice for poor families to sell their daughters to the wealthy, and these children spend their lives as laborers who receive no pay, only sustenance. The families of these girls aren't evil; they love their daughters but cannot afford to feed them or the rest of their families. This is the only way for them to survive.

For the cost of about $50 a year, Ms. Murray and the people she works with can provide a poor Nepalese family enough of what they need so that they can keep their children free. Imagine: fifty dollars to keep a girl out of slavery.

How fulfilling would it be to get a group of women to work toward staying healthy and losing weight together, while also raising money to keep children out of slavery and with their families?

Or do it on your own! If you choose to donate $5 for every pound you lose, once you reach ten pounds, you've *saved* a girl from a lifetime of servitude. Isn't that incredible? There are stories like this one all over the world. Find your own and get inspired!

*"Never doubt that a small group of committed citizens
can change the world. Indeed, it's the only thing that has."*

— Margaret Mead

The number of ways to help others is endless. I know it sounds corny, but how about baking a cake for a new neighbor? What if you bring over a roasted chicken to someone who's grieving, or some homemade jam to the folks who live next door? Sometimes reaching out to others with home cooking is the most personal and intimate way to connect. And that spirit of connecting with others may really help you stay conscious about what the role of food should be.

Finding a way to give back can engage your mind and body and your love of food in a way that broadens your own definition of what it means to be human and alive. Your life is precious; here's a way to show the world that you're grateful for, and respectful of, your place in the larger community.

Epilogue

*"'Who are you?' said the caterpillar. This was
not an encouraging opening for a conversation.
Alice replied, rather shyly, 'I—I hardly know,
Sir, just at present—at least I know who I was
when I got up this morning, but I think I must
have changed several times since then.'"*

— from *Alice's Adventures in Wonderland*
by Lewis Carroll

Changing our behavior is one of the hardest things we can choose to do. Our patterns are often so ingrained that it takes a jackhammer to loosen them. But I've always been overly optimistic about the human condition and its possibilities.

I hope that somewhere in this book, some little nugget jumped out at you and sparked an epiphany. If nothing else, perhaps you got a good laugh at how bizarre we've all become over our health.

You may have a lot of wishes about how you want to look, feel, and be. But a personal transformation isn't a concrete event; rather, it's a culmination of many smaller changes. You didn't gain weight overnight, or became unfit and stressed out in a week. You did it over a period of time. Take that into consideration, and try to reverse the process in the same way in which you created the problem.

Over the years, I can't begin to tell you how much of my time has been invested in obsessing over being the "right" weight, or the amount of money I've spent trying to acquire the "right" stuff that would help—things like packaged meals in boxes. But I had to think outside the box! Relentless exercising didn't help, either; I'd get more and more frustrated and mad at myself because I couldn't sustain it. Then I'd go back to my old eating habits and eventually start over again: "Maybe Slim-Fast would work . . . but I like to chew! How 'bout NutriSystem?"

However, I soon realized that I have less time ahead of me than I have behind me, and I didn't want to waste any more time (or money) investing in products and programs that were ultimately going to fail. So now I've adopted a healthy lifestyle. To me, that includes purchasing foods which, as author Michael Pollan says, will rot eventually. I don't eat to reduce stress. I exercise moderately and wisely—and I enjoy the process.

When I recently saw my old friend and colleague Miriam Nelson, who's the director of the John Hancock Center for Physical Activity and Nutrition at Tufts University, I asked her jokingly, "Do I look like Ms. Slenderella?" She responded, "Do you feel healthy and fit? That's all that you should be asking yourself."

One of the wisest ways to transition from where you are to where you want to be is to do it in baby steps. *Every* step toward being healthier and more fit is one that leads you toward your goal. Success breeds success . . . and failure leads to failure. So start small and keep at it!

When you follow this mind-set, you'll have a much greater chance in reaching your goals. Here are five benefits to taking baby steps:

1. *Make gradual changes to allow your underlying beliefs to shift with you.* Remember that everyone lives with thinking models that oppose one another. I call it "Twisted Sister and the Fairy Godmother." Your fairy godmother wants the best for you, but your twisted sister is always there to give you a good dose of fear and reasons why you shouldn't rock the boat. But the small actions you take to encourage the good impulses will make them stronger.

2. *Take small steps to give the people around you a chance to adjust.* The more gradual the change, the less likely you'll be to encounter resistance. (And maybe you'll gain some extra support, too.)

3. *Don't say too much about what your plans are for change.* You don't want people saying, in one way or another, "Oh, sure, I've heard that before!" It will only aggravate you, and who needs more stress?

4. *Make it a game.* Becoming healthy and fit is fun. Don't make the process into something that feels like you're preparing for war. If it doesn't always work for you, so what? Try, try again.

5. *Keep discussing what you want to happen—not what you <u>don't</u> want to happen.* Focusing on what you don't want only helps to create more of it. Write down what you want; see it in

your mind's eye; and practice, practice, practice. Eventually, your behavior will catch up. Just don't give up!

And remember . . . *have fun!*

Resources

Books That Make Sense

Animal, Vegetable, Miracle: A Year of Food Life, Barbara Kingsolver, with Steven L. Hopp and Camille Kingsolver. New York: HarperCollins, 2007.

Be Happy Without Being Perfect: How to Break Free from the Perfection Deception, Alice D. Domar, Ph.D., and Alice Lesch Kelly. New York: Crown Publishers, 2008.

The Biology of Belief: Unleashing the Power of Consciousness, Matter & Miracles, Bruce H. Lipton, Ph.D. Carlsbad, CA: Hay House, Inc., 2008.

The End of Stress as We Know It, Bruce McEwen, with Elizabeth Norton Lasley. Washington, D.C.: Joseph Henry Press, 2002.

Good Calories, Bad Calories: Fats, Carbs, and the Controversial Science of Diet and Health, Gary Taubes. New York: Anchor Books, 2008.

In Defense of Food: An Eater's Manifesto, Michael Pollan. New York: Penguin Press, 2008.

Loneliness: Human Nature and the Need for Social Connection, John T. Cacioppo and William Patrick. New York: W. W. Norton & Company, Inc., 2008.

Medical Myths That Can Kill You: And the 101 Truths That Will Save, Extend, and Improve Your Life, Nancy L. Snyderman, M.D. New York: Crown Publishers, 2008.

Spark: The Revolutionary New Science of Exercise and the Brain, John Ratey, M.D., with Eric Hagerman. New York: Little, Brown and Company, 2008.

Stretching: 20th Anniversary Revised Edition, Bob Anderson. Bolinas, CA: Shelter Publications, Inc., 2000.

Strong Women and Men Beat Arthritis, Miriam E. Nelson, Ph.D.; Kristin R. Baker, Ph.D.; and Ronenn Roubenoff, M.D., M.H.S.; with Lawrence Lindner, M.A. New York: G. P. Putnam's Sons, 2002.

Strong Women Eat Well, Miriam E. Nelson, Ph.D., with Judy Knipe. New York: G. P. Putnam's Sons, 2001.

Why Men Die First: How to Lengthen Your Lifespan, Marianne J. Legato, M.D., F.A.C.P. New York: Palgrave Macmillan, 2008.

Websites

BeWell (www.bewell.com)

America's leading health experts have come together to launch a Website to provide more reliable information and guidance concerning health issues. Hosted by Dr. Nancy Snyderman, chief medical editor at NBC News, BeWell is the first social network based on online discussions with advice and support from leading physicians and health-care professionals. Well-known experts include Dr. Susan Love, breast-cancer surgeon; Dr. Miriam Nelson, fitness and nutrition; Dr. Marianne Legato, gender scientist/internist; and many others . . . including me, Loretta LaRoche!

Health Journeys (www.healthjourneys.com)

Health Journeys produces and distributes products that teach healing and wellness practices such as guided imagery and meditation. Audio programs, books, and additional products are available on topics including stress relief, weight loss and fitness, pain management, general well-being, and many others.

Acknowledgments

Thanks to my family of origin for instilling in me a love of laughter and food. I can't think of a better way to go through life. To Louise Hay, for being a master visionary; to Reid Tracy, the president of Hay House, for his confidence in me as an author; to editors Jill Kramer and Lisa Mitchell; to Brian DeFiore, my literary agent and co-conspirator; and to all of you who have attended my lectures, read my books, or watched my PBS specials. May you live long, happy lives and eat well every day.

About the Author

Loretta LaRoche, the best-selling author of *Life Is Short—Wear Your Party Pants* and *Squeeze the Day,* among other works, is a stress-management consultant who advocates humor, optimism, and resiliency as coping mechanisms. She uses her wit and wisdom to help people learn how to take stress and turn it into strength, and how to see themselves as the survivors of their own lives—that is, to find the "bless in the mess."

Loretta is a favorite with viewers of her PBS specials, as well as on the lecture circuit, where she presents an average of 100 talks per year. She lives in Plymouth, Massachusetts.

Website: **www.LorettaLaroche.com**

Hay House Titles of Related Interest

YOU CAN HEAL YOUR LIFE, *the movie,* starring Louise L. Hay & Friends
(available as a 1-DVD program and an expanded 2-DVD set)
Watch the trailer at: **www.LouiseHayMovie.com**

THE SHIFT, *the movie,* starring Dr. Wayne W. Dyer
(available as a 1-DVD program and an expanded 2-DVD set)
Watch the trailer at: **www.DyerMovie.com**

THE ART OF EXTREME SELF-CARE: *Transform Your Life*
One Month at a Time, by Cheryl Richardson

THE BIOLOGY OF BELIEF: *Unleashing the Power*
of Consciousness, Matter & Miracles, by Bruce Lipton, Ph.D.

THE BODY KNOWS . . . HOW TO STAY YOUNG: *Healthy-Aging Secrets*
from a Medical Intuitive, by Caroline Sutherland

CREATING INNER HARMONY: *Using Your Voice and Music to Heal*
(book-with-CD), by Don Campbell

EVERYTHING YOU NEED TO KNOW TO FEEL GO(O)D,
by Candace B. Pert, Ph.D., with Nancy Marriott

EXCUSES BEGONE! *How to Change Lifelong,*
Self-Defeating Thinking Habits, by Dr. Wayne W. Dyer

RECIPES FOR HEALTH BLISS: *Using NatureFoods & Lifestyle Choices*
to Rejuvenate Your Body & Life, by Susan Smith Jones, Ph.D.

SAYING YES TO CHANGE: *Essential Wisdom for Your Journey*
(book-with-CD), by Joan Z. Borysenko, Ph.D., and Gordon F. Dveirin

THE SECRET PLEASURES OF MENOPAUSE, by Christiane Northrup, M.D.

SIMPLY . . . WOMAN! *The 12-Week Body/Mind/Soul Total Transformation*
Program, New and Revised Edition! (book-with-DVD), by Crystal Andrus

All of the above are available at your local bookstore,
or may be ordered by contacting Hay House (see last page).

We hope you enjoyed this Hay House book. If you'd like to
receive our online catalog featuring additional information
on Hay House books and products, or if you'd like to find
out more about the Hay Foundation, please contact:

Hay House, Inc.
P.O. Box 5100
Carlsbad, CA 92018-5100

(760) 431-7695 or **(800) 654-5126**
(760) 431-6948 (fax) or **(800) 650-5115 (fax)**
www.hayhouse.com® • **www.hayfoundation.org**

Published and distributed in Australia by: Hay House Australia Pty. Ltd.,
18/36 Ralph St., Alexandria NSW 2015 • *Phone:* 612-9669-4299
Fax: 612-9669-4144 • www.hayhouse.com.au

Published and distributed in the United Kingdom by: Hay House UK, Ltd.,
292B Kensal Rd., London W10 5BE • *Phone:* 44-20-8962-1230
Fax: 44-20-8962-1239 • www.hayhouse.co.uk

Published and distributed in the Republic of South Africa by: Hay House SA
(Pty), Ltd., P.O. Box 990, Witkoppen 2068 • *Phone/Fax:* 27-11-467-8904
orders@psdprom.co.za • www.hayhouse.co.za

Published in India by: Hay House Publishers India, Muskaan Complex,
Plot No. 3, B-2, Vasant Kunj, New Delhi 110 070 • *Phone:* 91-11-4176-1620
Fax: 91-11-4176-1630 • www.hayhouse.co.in

Distributed in Canada by: Raincoast, 9050 Shaughnessy St.,
Vancouver, B.C. V6P 6E5 • *Phone:* (604) 323-7100
Fax: (604) 323-2600 • www.raincoast.com

Take Your Soul on a Vacation

Visit **www.HealYourLife.com**® to regroup,
recharge, and reconnect with your own magnificence.
Featuring blogs, mind-body-spirit news, and
life-changing wisdom from Louise Hay and friends.

Visit **www.HealYourLife.com** today!

HAY HOUSE

Tune in to Hay House Radio to listen to your favorite authors: **HayHouseRadio.com**®

Yes, I'd like to receive:

☐ **a Hay House catalog**   ☐ *The Louise Hay Newsletter*
☐ *The Christiane Northrup Newsletter*   ☐ *The Sylvia Browne Newsletter*

Name _____

Address _____

City _____ State _____ Zip _____

E-mail _____

Also, please send:

☐ **a Hay House catalog**   ☐ *The Louise Hay Newsletter*
☐ *The Christiane Northrup Newsletter*   ☐ *The Sylvia Browne Newsletter*

To:
Name _____

Address _____

City _____ State _____ Zip _____

E-mail _____

To:

HAY HOUSE, INC.
P.O. Box 5100
Carlsbad, CA 92018-5100

Place
Stamp
Here